Words of Others
Blackout Poetry

Holly Wells

FOREWORD BY MEG AINSWORTH

D1566597

WORDS OF OTHERS

BLACKOUT POETRY

WRITTEN AND ARRANGED BY **HOLLY WELLS**

FOREWORD BY MEG AINSWORTH

ALL RIGHTS RESERVED.

INITIAL COVER ART BY ROBERT MAGEE

COVER DESIGN BY MITCH GREEN

Words of Others

Blackout Poetry

Dedication

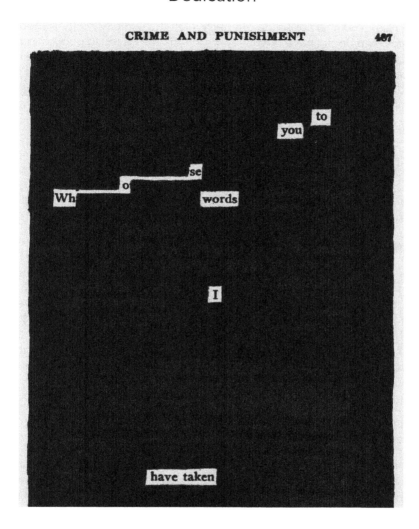

and in memory of my grandmother, Estelle Andrews Ellington, from whom I inherited a love of words, and of my grandfather, Guy Milloy Magee, from whom I inherited a love of history

Foreword

When I first read this collection of poetry, I felt the same way I feel when I happen across a book I have never seen. One that has been in publication for decades, or for centuries even, and is so illuminating that I am astonished I have never seen it before. Often these texts are found in yellowing book shops that smell of dust and paper, the true home of readers hungry for a wealth invisible to the rest of the world.

Words of Others is one of those books.

Poets are incredibly brave beings. Their art is rich with life. They write about subjects that other writers would not dare touch *and* they do it eloquently and gracefully, just as Holly Wells does in this collection. Blackout poetry is a young genre, but an incredibly smart one. What blackout poets do is, quite literally, scratch through the surface of texts to the living, vibrating, electric undercurrent of language. Blackout poets, like expert sculptors, carve through the expectations of texts to the poetry beneath it all.

Words of Others takes both literary and theological texts, from Jane Austen to Jonathan Edwards, and not only gives voices to the silenced, but re-writes history. If the ideas of synchronicity and connectivity are right, and I believe they are, then the poems in this book speak both for those who have been historically marginalized, as well as for those of us who cannot find words enough to express elements of our own souls. Poet-oracles, such as the author of this book, thank God, have always been scattered throughout cultures and across boundaries of time to both engage and connect with.

What you now hold in your hands is both a black-listed version of history and a searching through layers of text to the nameless song that echoes from the collective soul of all of humanity.

The black spaces surrounding the poems in this book stole my attention from the start, and I imagined the millions of scratches it takes to darken some words in order to see others, revealing a shining skeleton of a poem in the midst of the dark. Poems are ever before us, they have always been buried deep beneath culture and oppression and the buzzing static of everyday life. It takes poet-prophets to unearth them like fossils and offer them up on pages such as these.

These are stories untold. These are bones unsatisfied in their bound caskets, rising at the recognition of words and shaking off the tired rust of centuries.

Words of Others is a kind of home for people who have a hunch about the ruse of society, people who walk through their days, shading False for Real fifty times by noon.

Poetry, we know, seeks to "say the unsayable." No book or essay or piece of prose, no matter its length or grandiosity, can ever really say what it means. Only poetry can do that and it can only do it through signifiers, symbols like candlelight and mists and cathedrals in this very text.

A cathedral is never a cathedral. Language always falls short. "Cathedral" is every bit of what is meant by it, though--a house for God, like a body, a hinged chest concealing what is holy, the ultimate unspeakable paradox. Poets smash the cathedral to pieces and offer up the mystery of it all.

"Here," the poet says, "take and eat."

The following work is the same transcendent mystery that lingers in ancient spaces. This book is not only a neon sunset to a blind world, but is also its own metaphor. It is a way to see the world through murky waters, through the clouded sky, to what is true. Few have been given eyes to see that way. The world, and the writing world included, is starving for the feast that poets have foraged from what most can only see as a trash heap.

So, here are the riches of a poet who has rummaged for mirrors and found truth. Here are the diamonds for those whose eyes have not been dulled.

Here: Light.

Meg Ainsworth

Table of Contents

Out of Darkness, Light   13

Literature in Brief   53

True Life   97

Silenced Voices   145

True Love   171

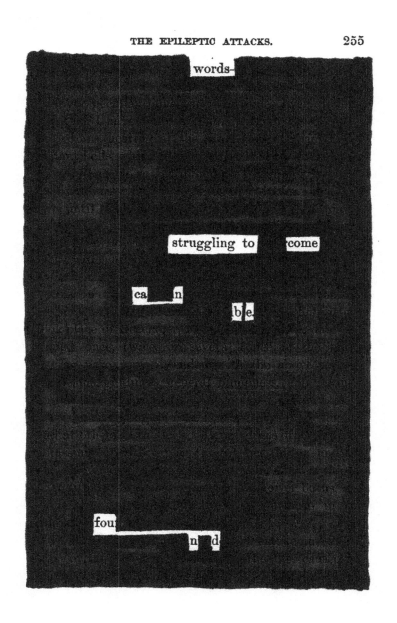

words—

struggling to come

ca n

b e

fou n d

A Defense of Blackout Poetry

11

Part One

███████████ out ██████
Of ████████████████████
██████████████ darkness,
██████ light ████████████

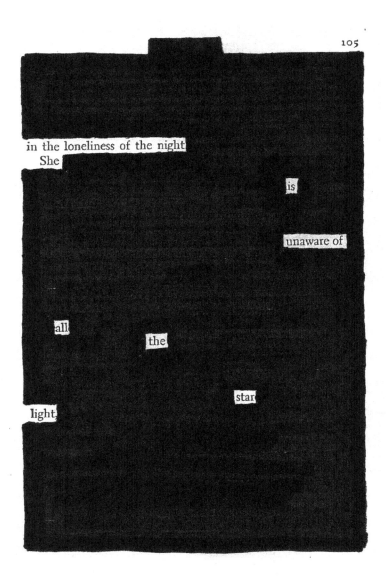

in the loneliness of the night
She

is

unaware of

all

the

star

light.

Loneliness

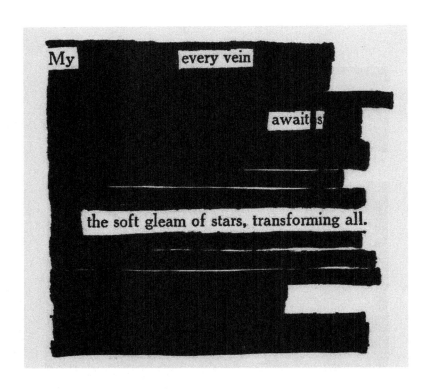

My

every vein

await s

the soft gleam of stars, transforming all.

My Every Vein

from Rainer Maria Rilke

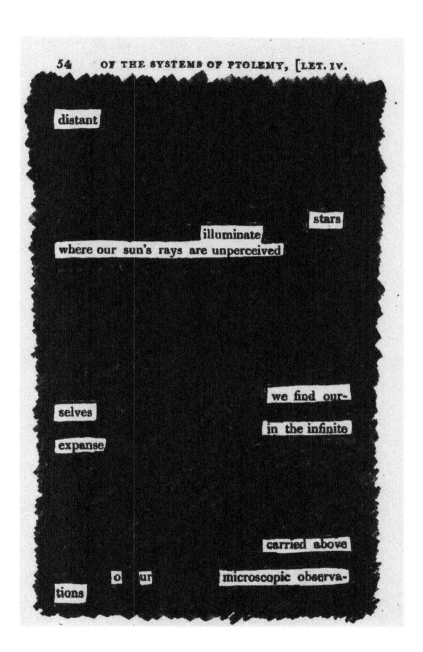

distant

stars

illuminate
where our sun's rays are unperceived

we find our-

selves

in the infinite

expanse

carried above

o   ur   microscopic observa-
tions

Considering the Stars

17

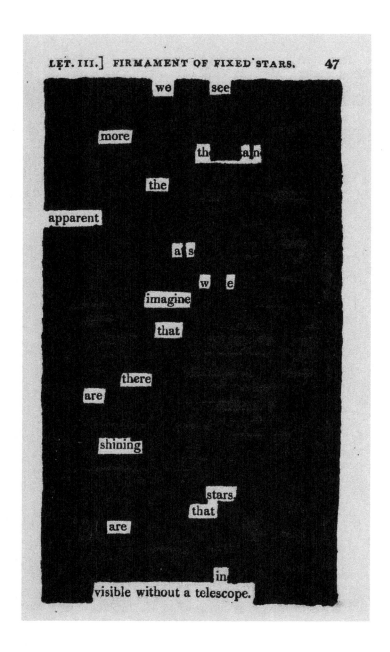

Considering the Stars II

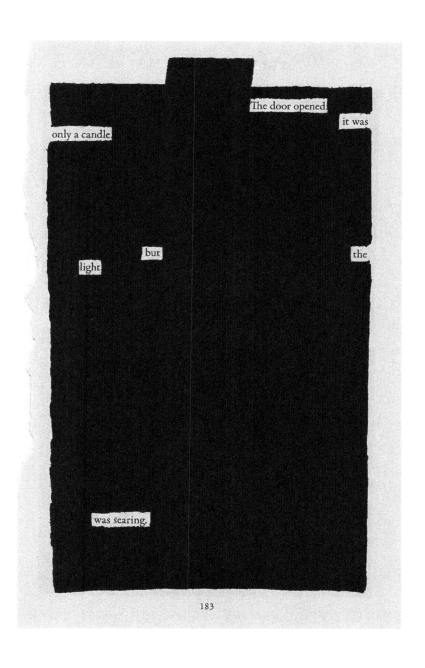

The door opened. it was

only a candle.

but the

light

was searing.

183

Only a Candle

19

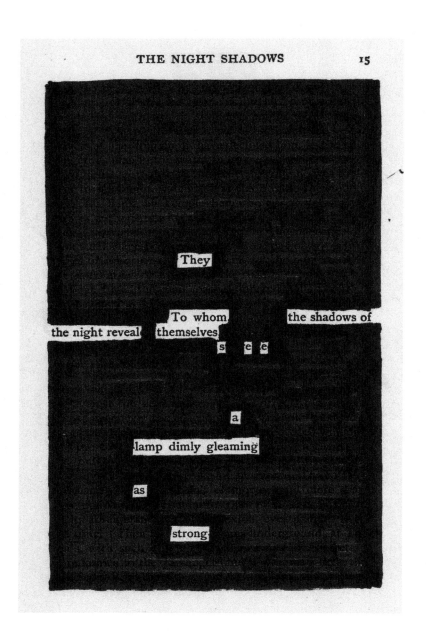

They

To whom the shadows of
the night reveal themselves

s e e

a

lamp dimly gleaming

as

strong

Night Shadows

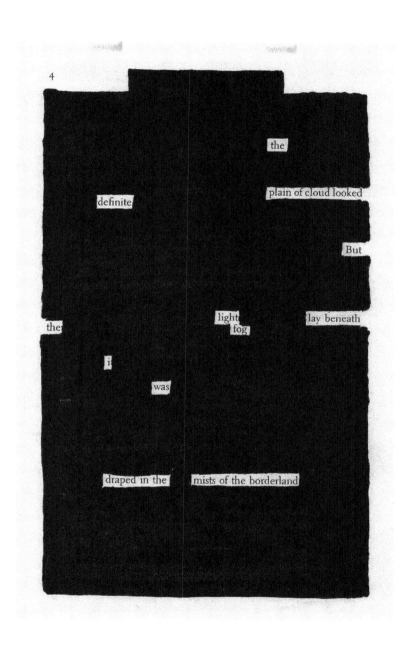

4

the

plain of cloud looked

definite

But

the

light
fog

lay beneath

i

was

draped in the   mists of the borderland

The Mists of the Borderland

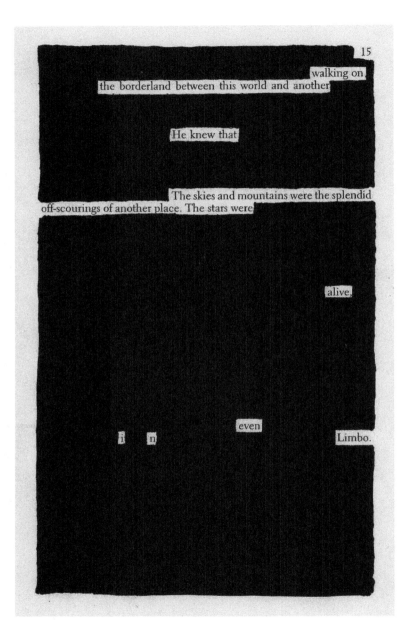

walking on the borderland between this world and another

He knew that

The skies and mountains were the splendid off-scourings of another place. The stars were

alive.

i n even Limbo.

Even in Limbo

NIGHT

Night
from C. S. Lewis's Spirits in Bondage

DUNGEON GRATES

████ hope undone. ████████████████████

████ in █ o █

██████████████ light ██████

To lead you out ██████████

████████████████████████

Till ██████████████████████

████████████████████████

██████████ All things are seen aright

████████████████████████

████████████████████████

████████

████████████████████████

█ for one little moment ████████

████████████████████████

████████████████████████

████████████████████████

████ and ██████████████

████████████

████████████

████████████████████████

We know we are not made of mortal stuff.

Dungeon Grates
from C. S. Lewis's Spirits in Bondage

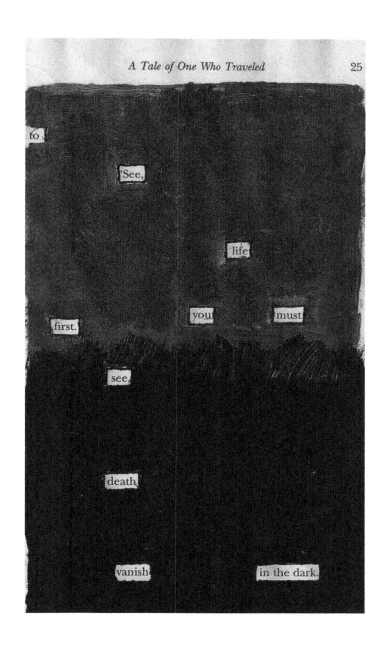

to

'See,

life

you must

first.

see.

death.

vanish

in the dark.

A Tale of One Who Traveled

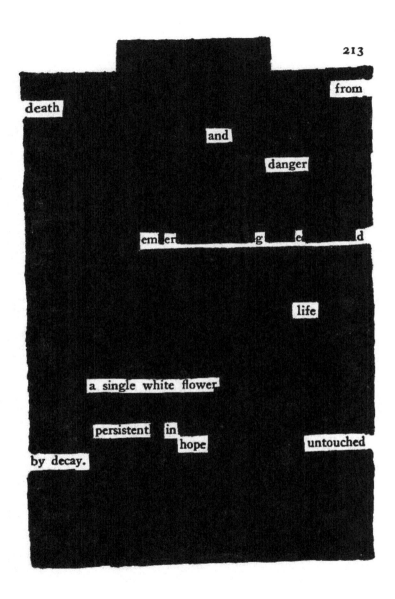

death

from

and

danger

em er g e d

life

a single white flower

persistent in
hope
untouched
by decay.

A Single White Flower

CHAPTER V.

AMPUTATIONS.

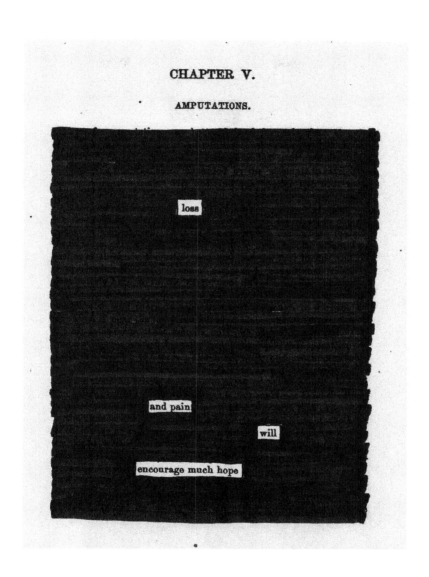

loss

and pain

will

encourage much hope

Amputations

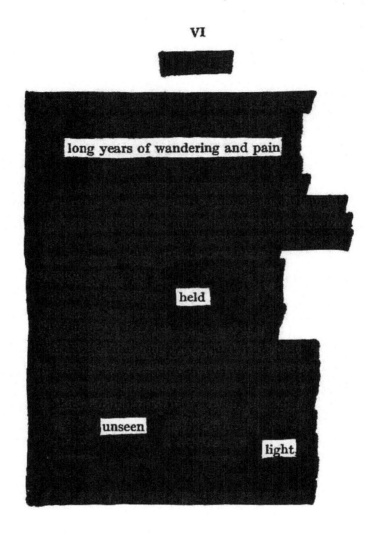

long years of wandering and pain

held

unseen

light.

Unseen Light
from C. S. Lewis's Spirits in Bondage

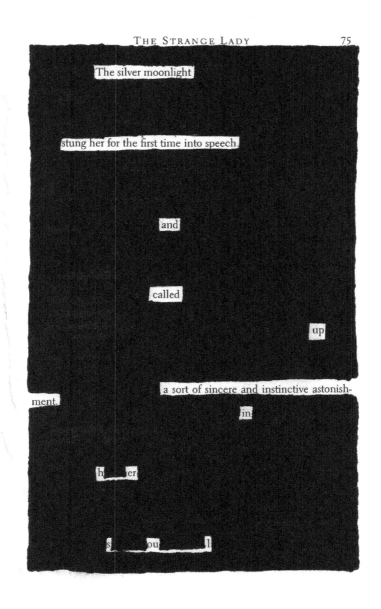

The silver moonlight

stung her for the first time into speech.

and

called

up

a sort of sincere and instinctive astonish-
ment.

in

h   er

s   ou   l

The Strange Lady, Part One

29

she remem-
bered herself

and was slowly awakening

like a tree.

reviving in
the middle of
w in
ter

The Strange Lady, Part Two

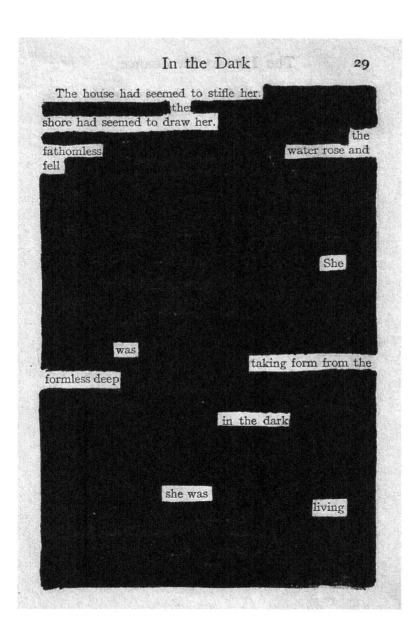

The house had seemed to stifle her.
the
shore had seemed to draw her.

the
fathomless   water rose and
fell

She

was

taking form from the
formless deep

in the dark

she was

living

In the Dark

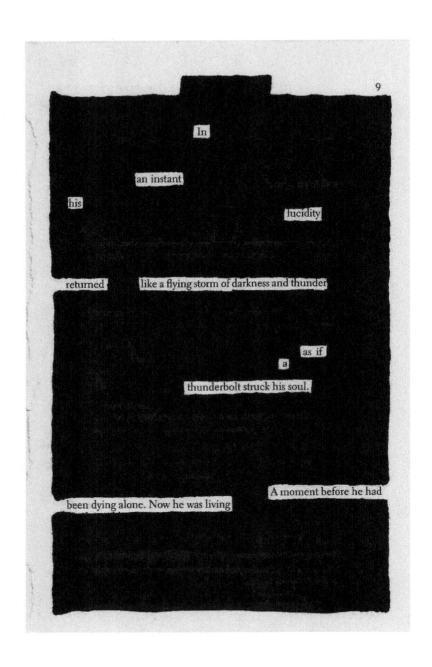

In

an instant

his   lucidity

returned   like a flying storm of darkness and thunder

                                                        as if
                                              a

                              thunderbolt struck his soul.

                                                  A moment before he had
              been dying alone. Now he was living

Now He Was Living

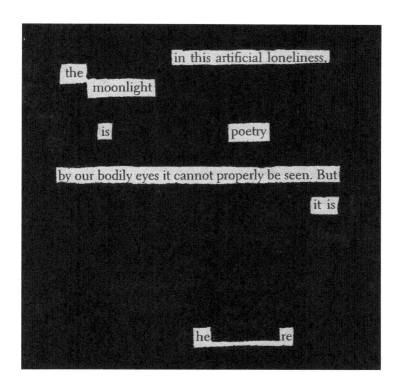

in this artificial loneliness,
the
moonlight

is   poetry

by our bodily eyes it cannot properly be seen. But

it is

he   re

The Moonlight Is Poetry

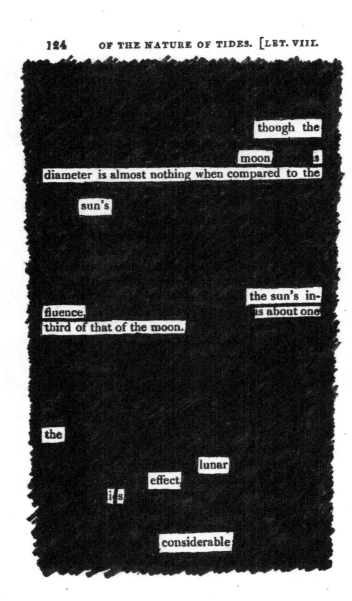

though the
moon   s
diameter is almost nothing when compared to the
sun's

the sun's in-
fluence.   is about one
third of that of the moon.

the

lunar
effect
i s

considerable

Lunar Effect

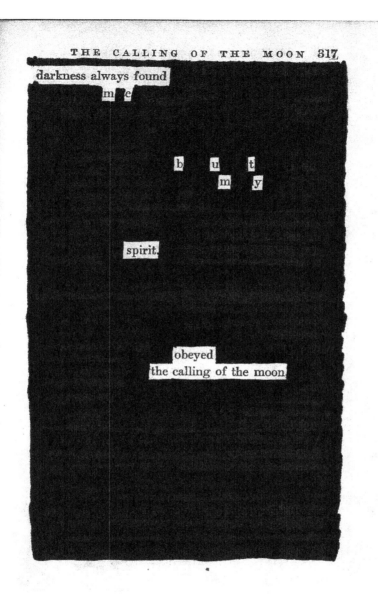

darkness always found
m e

b   u   t
        m   y

spirit.

obeyed
the calling of the moon.

The Calling of the Moon

35

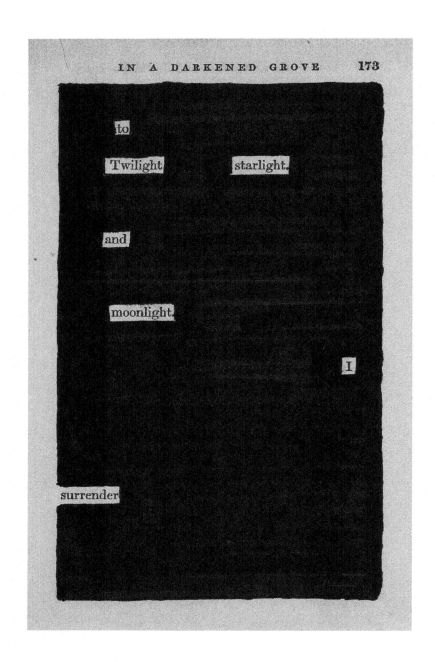

In a Darkened Grove

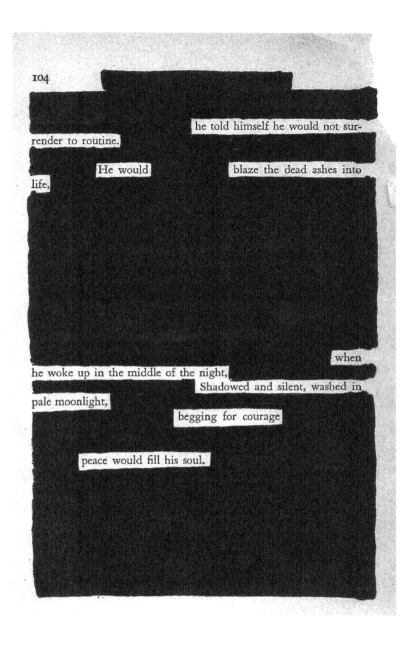

he told himself he would not sur-
render to routine.

He would blaze the dead ashes into
life,

when
he woke up in the middle of the night,
Shadowed and silent, washed in
pale moonlight,

begging for courage

peace would fill his soul.

Blaze the Dead Ashes

37

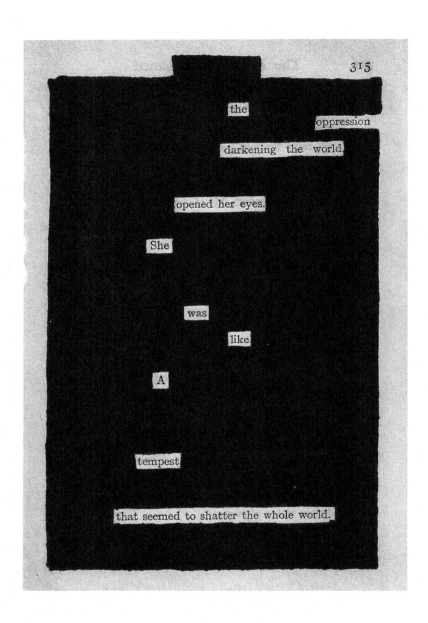

the

oppression

darkening the world.

opened her eyes.

She

was

like

A

tempest

that seemed to shatter the whole world.

Shatter the World

The Lunatic Asylum

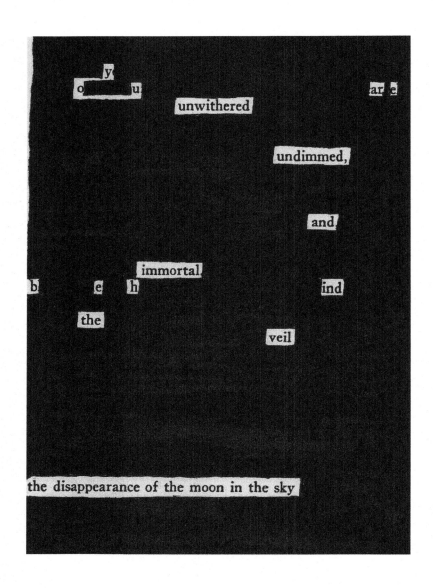

o y o u   ar e

unwithered

undimmed,

and

immortal
b   e   h   ind

the

veil

the disappearance of the moon in the sky

The Soul Refined

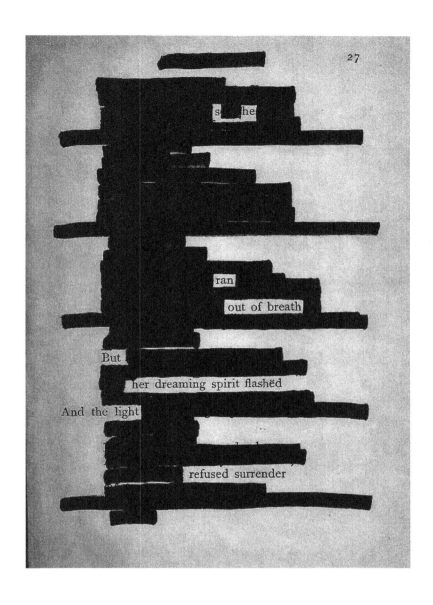

Dreaming Spirit

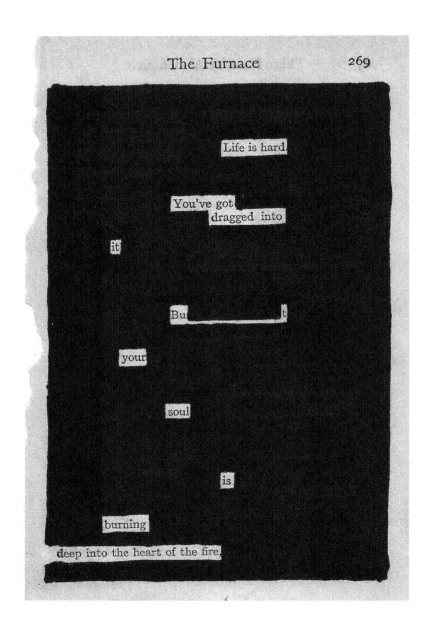

Life is hard.

You've got
dragged into

it

Bu_____t

your

soul

is

burning

deep into the heart of the fire,

The Furnace

42

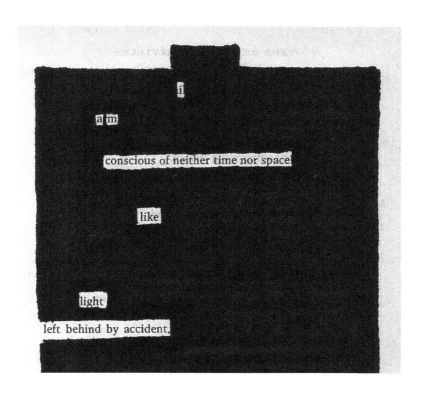

i

a m

conscious of neither time nor space

like

light

left behind by accident.

Consciousness

DE PROFUNDIS

Even if █████████████████████████
████████████████████████████████
████████████████████████████████
████████████████████████████████
████████████████████████████████
████████████████████████████████
dungeons and deep cells █████████
████████████████ art ███ strong.
████████████████████████████████
████████████████████████████████
████████████████████████████████
████████████████████████████████
████████████████████████████████
this frail, bruised being is █████
██████████ thirsting ████████████
████████ seeking ████████████████
████████████ relentless █████████
████████████████████████████████
████████████████████████████████
████████████████████████████████

34

De Profundis
from C. S. Lewis's Spirits in Bondage

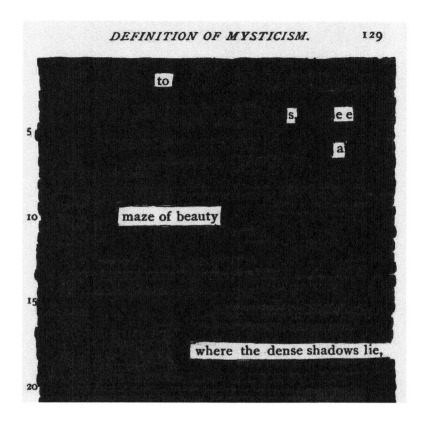

Definition of Mysticism

45

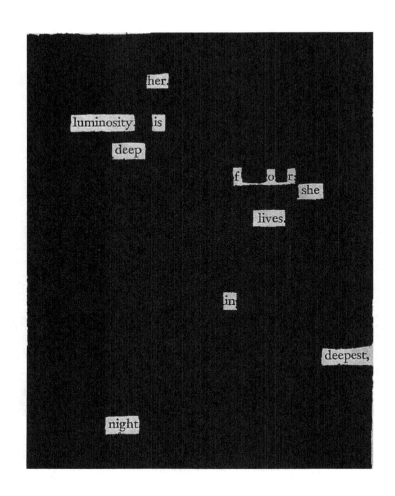

Deep Luminosity

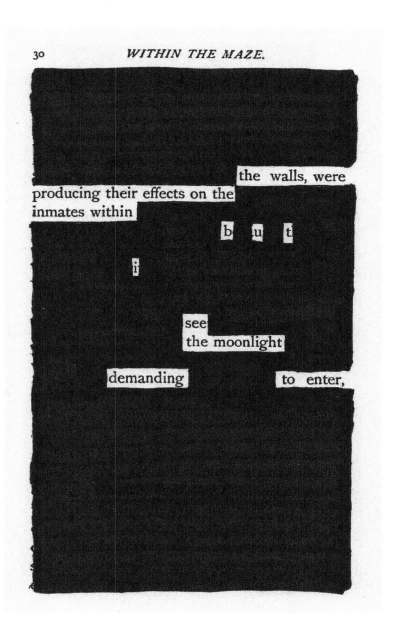

the walls, were
producing their effects on the
inmates within

b u t

i

see
the moonlight

demanding   to enter,

Within the Maze

47

Walls Dissolved

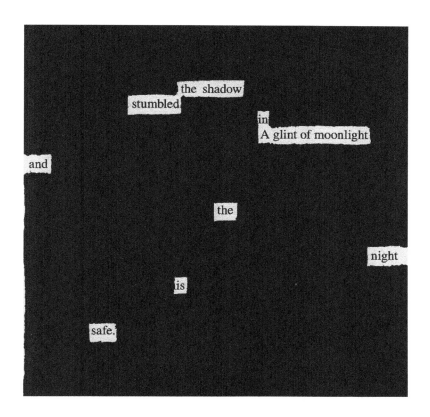

the shadow
stumbled
in
A glint of moonlight

and

the

night

is

safe.

49

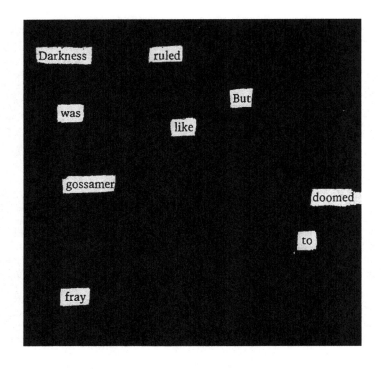

Doomed to Fray

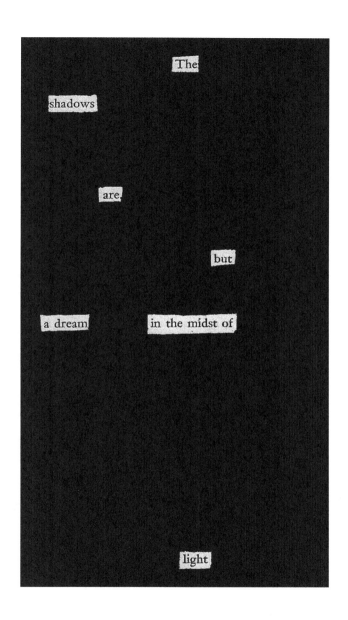

The

shadows

are,

but

a dream   in the midst of

light

A Dream in the Midst of Light

as
darkness fell, my overshadowing dread

mastered me.

but

after that,

a veil seemed
to be drawn from the river, and millions of sparkles burst out

The Morning Dawns

52

Part Two

 literature in brief.

Hamlet

William Shakespeare

The

foul and fair

are

not　　　　a　s　　40

you

interpret

50

Macbeth
William Shakespeare

58

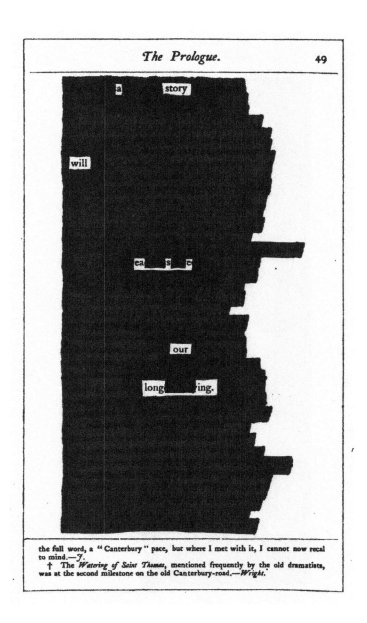

a story

will

ea s c

our

long ing.

the full word, a " Canterbury " pace, but where I met with it, I cannot now recal to mind.—*J*.

† The *Watering of Saint Thomas*, mentioned frequently by the old dramatists, was at the second milestone on the old Canterbury-road.—*Wright.*

The Canterbury Tales

Geoffrey Chaucer

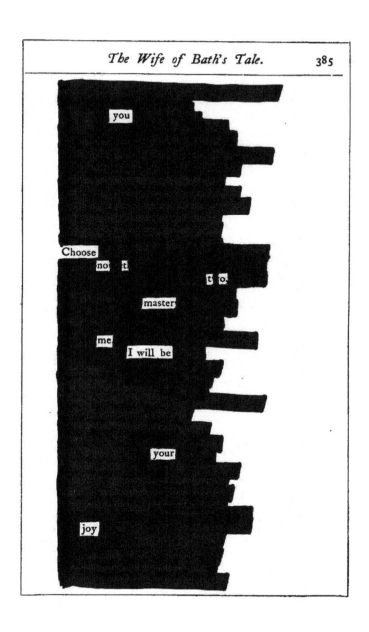

The Wife of Bath's Tale

Geoffrey Chaucer

THE INFERNO.

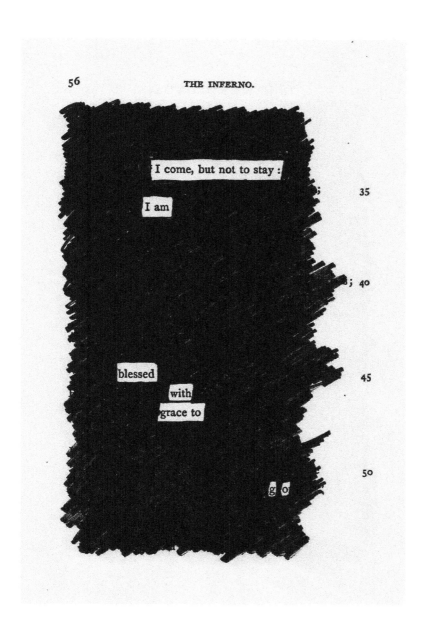

I come, but not to stay :

35

I am

; 40

blessed

45

with
grace to

50

g o

Divine Comedy: Inferno

Dante

61

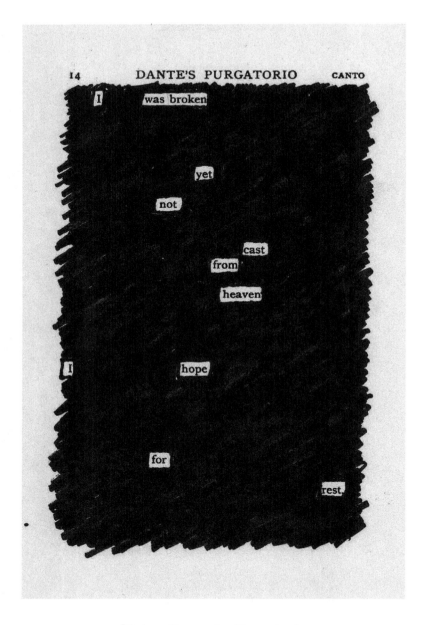

Divine Comedy: Purgatorio
Dante

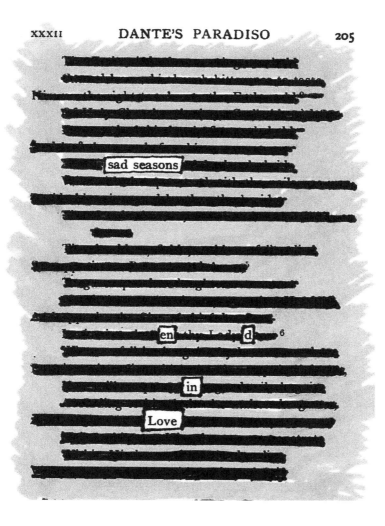

sad seasons

en d 6

in

Love

Divine Comedy: Paradiso
Dante

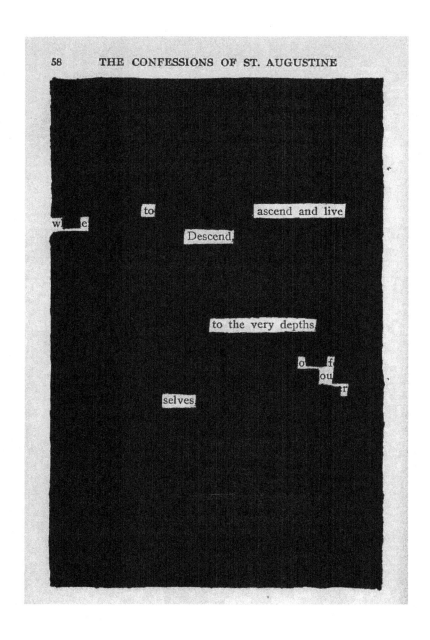

to   ascend and live
w   e
        Descend.

            to the very depths
                        o   f
                        ou
                            r
    selves.

Confessions

Augustine of Hippo

64

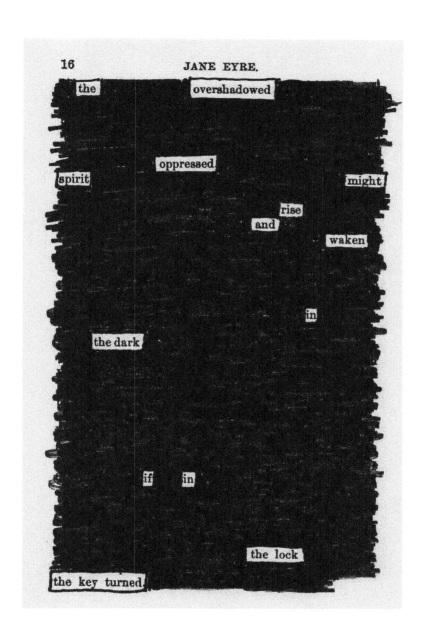

the

overshadowed

oppressed.

spirit

might

rise

and

waken

in

the dark

if in

the lock

the key turned

Jane Eyre, Part One

Charlotte Brontë

65

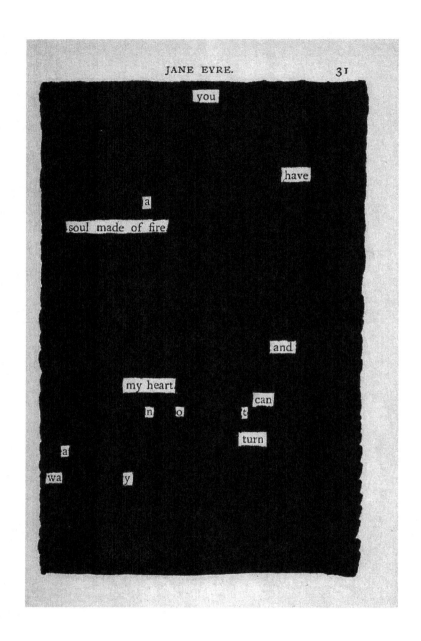

you

have

a

soul made of fire

and

my heart

n   o   t   can

turn

a

wa   y

Jane Eyre, Part Two

Charlotte Bronte

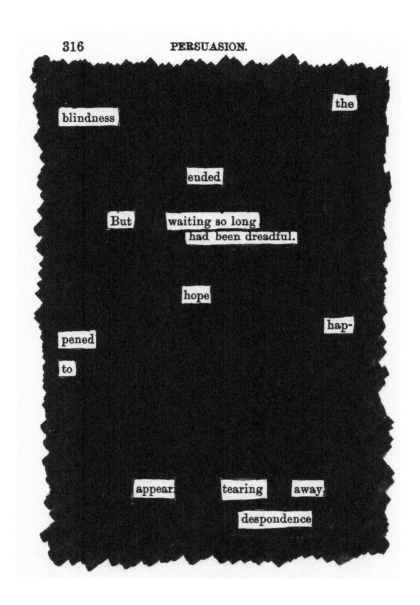

the

blindness

ended

But   waiting so long
         had been dreadful.

hope

hap-

pened

to

appear   tearing   away

despondence

Persuasion

Jane Austen

her

declaration,

of

love

came out quite unawares,

Sense and Sensibility

Jane Austen

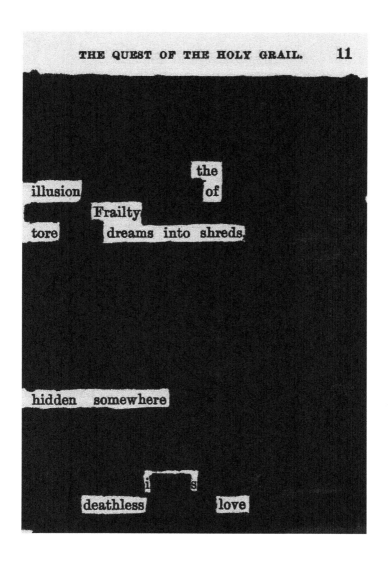

illusion the of
Frailty
tore dreams into shreds.

hidden somewhere

i s
deathless love

The Quest of the Holy Grail

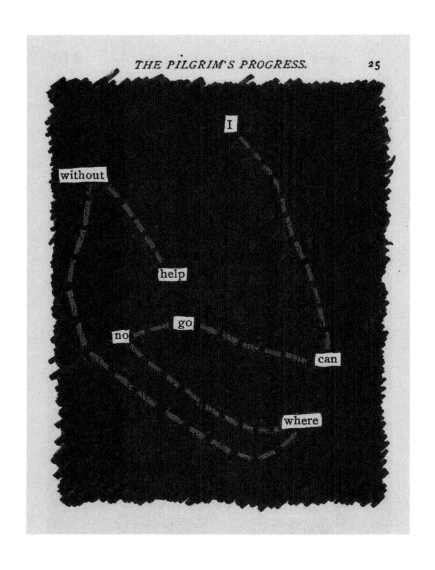

The Pilgrim's Progress
John Bunyan

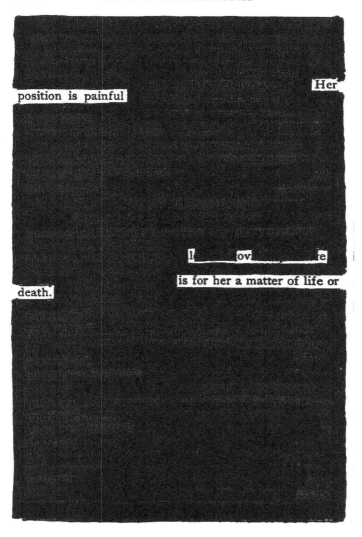

position is painful

Her

l ov e

is for her a matter of life or death.

Anna Karenina

Leo Tolstoy

71

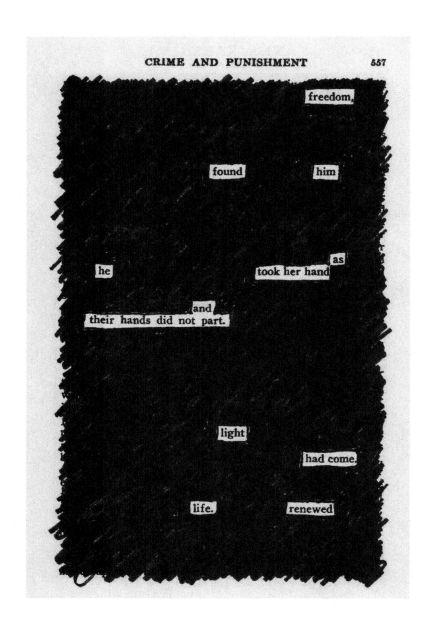

freedom,

found him

he took her hand as

and
their hands did not part.

light

had come.

life. renewed

Crime and Punishment
Fyodor Dostoyevsky

72

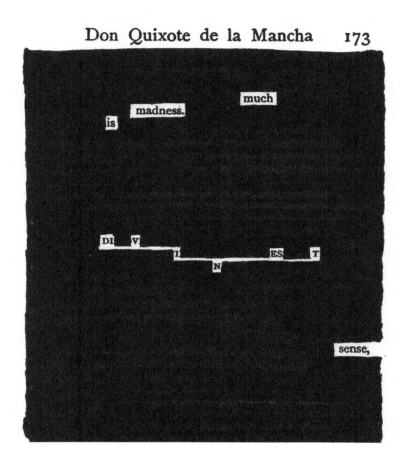

Don Quixote de la Mancha
Miguel de Cervantes

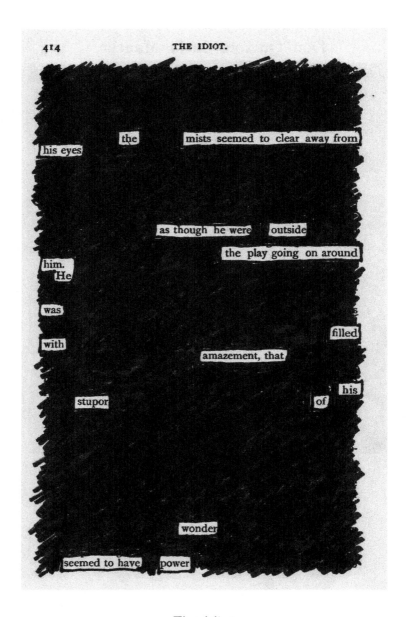

the   mists seemed to clear away from

his eyes

as though he were   outside

the play going on around

him.
He

was

filled

with

amazement, that

his

stupor   of

wonder

seemed to have   power

The Idiot

Fyodor Dostoyevsky

74

death

is

revealed,

blind eyes

see clear,

Oedipus the King

Sophocles

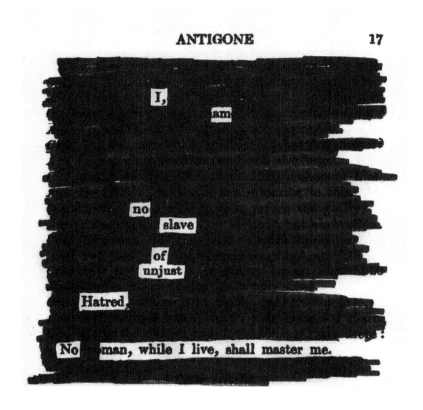

I,

am

no

slave

of

unjust

Hatred.

No man, while I live, shall master me.

Antigone

Sophocles

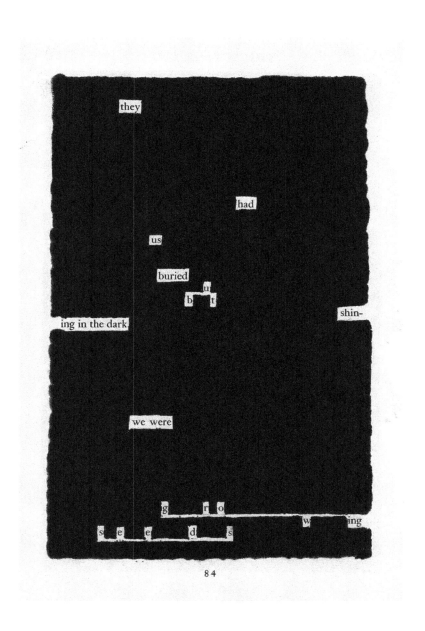

The Handmaid's Tale (in a Mexican Proverb)

Margaret Atwood

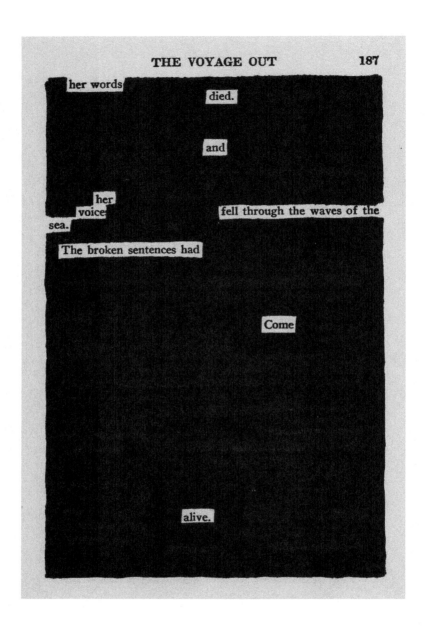

her words died. and her voices fell through the waves of the sea. The broken sentences had Come alive.

The Voyage Out
Virginia Woolf

78

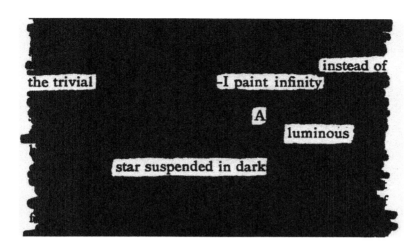

the trivial   -I paint infinity   instead of

A

luminous

star suspended in dark

The Letters of Vincent van Gogh

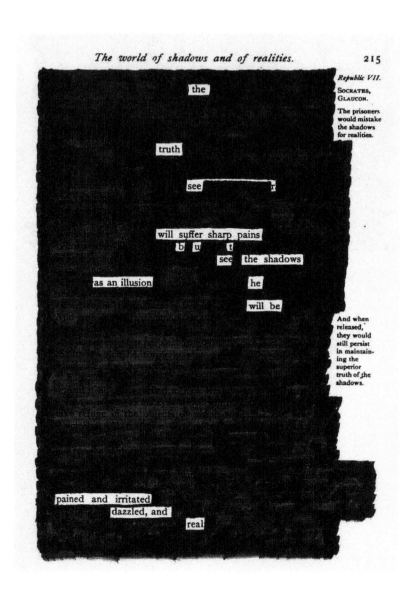

Republic VII.

SOCRATES,
GLAUCON.

The prisoners
would mistake
the shadows
for realities.

the

truth

see r

will suffer sharp pains
b u t
see the shadows

as an illusion he

will be

And when
released,
they would
still persist
in maintain-
ing the
superior
truth of the
shadows.

pained and irritated
dazzled, and
real

The Allegory of the Cave
Plato

80

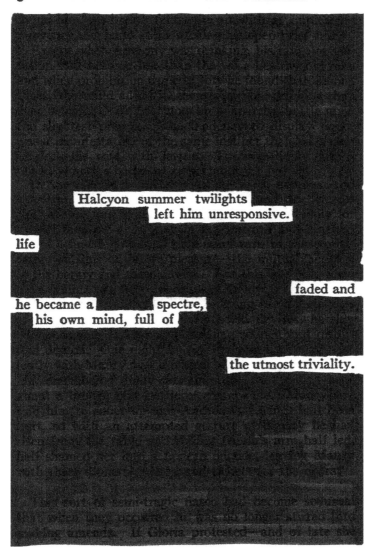

Halcyon summer twilights
left him unresponsive.

life

faded and

he became a spectre,
his own mind, full of

the utmost triviality.

The Beautiful and Damned, Part One
F. Scott Fitzgerald

81

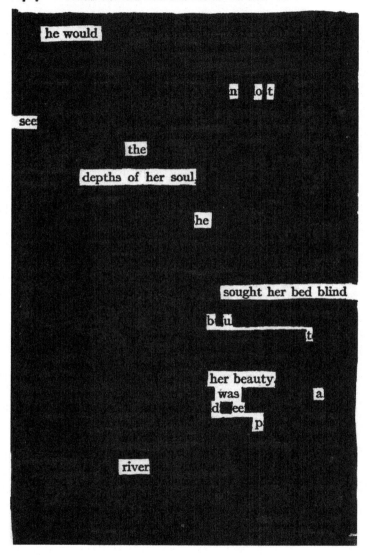

he would

n o t

see

the

depths of her soul.

he

sought her bed blind

b u t

her beauty was d ee p

a

river

The Beautiful and Damned, Part Two

F. Scott Fitzgerald

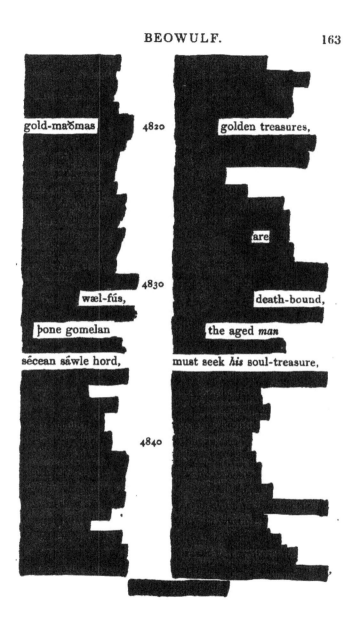

gold-maðmas 4820 golden treasures,

are

4830
wæl-fús, death-bound,

þone gomelan the aged *man*

sécean sáwle hord, must seek *his* soul-treasure,

4840

Beowulf's Flaw

83

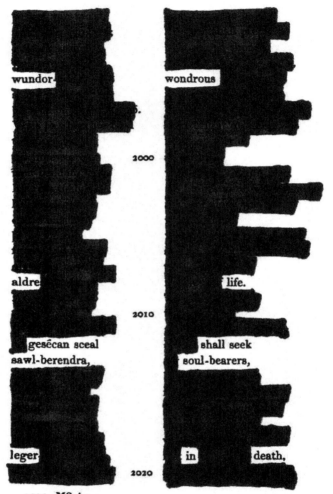

wundor-

wondrous

2000

aldre

life.

2010

gesécan sceal
sawl-berendra,

shall seek
soul-bearers,

leger

in death,

2020

2005. MS. þe.

2009–2020. These lines are extremely obscure: þæt (l. 2009) no doubt means *death*, implied in aldres orwêna.

2012. MS. gesacan.

Beowulf's Hope

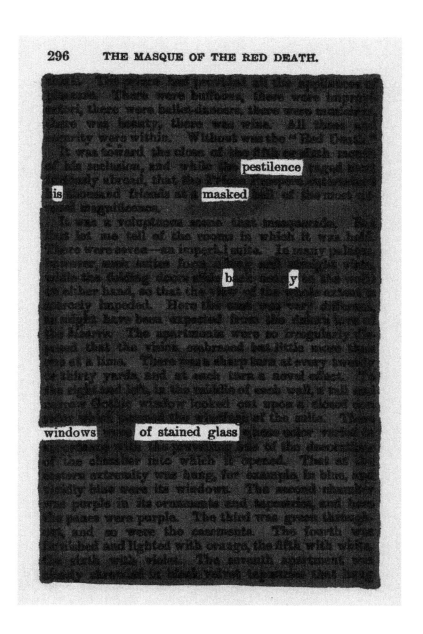

pestilence

is masked

b y

windows of stained glass

The Masque of the Red Death

Edgar Allan Poe

what

had been hidden

in the

:o p en·

the

poet

could

s e e

The Purloined Letter
Edgar Allan Poe

(60)

false

gifts

(70)

conceal

insidious death

and

(90)

grief overwhelms me.

The Iliad
Homer

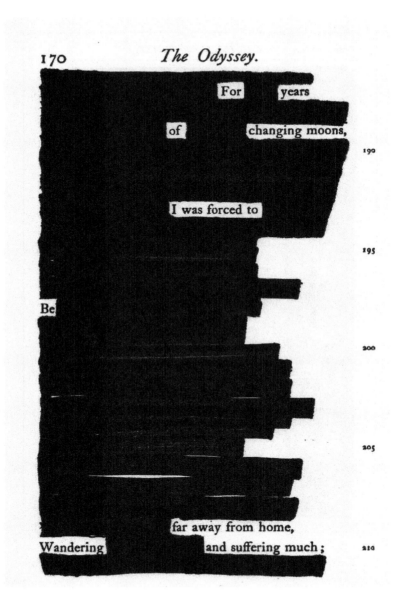

For   years

of   changing moons,

I was forced to

Be

far away from home,

Wandering   and suffering much;

The Odyssey
Homer

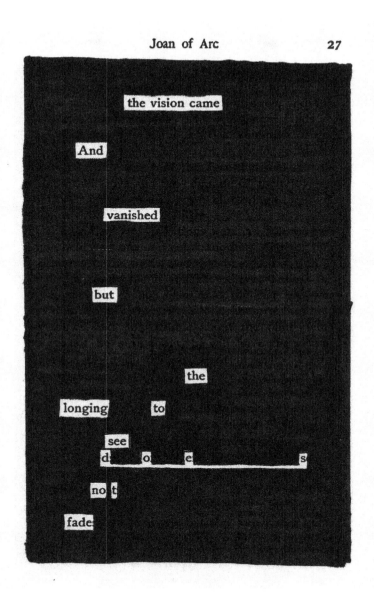

the vision came

And

vanished

but

the

longing   to

see

d: o   e   s

no t

fade

The Personal Recollections of Joan of Arc

Mark Twain

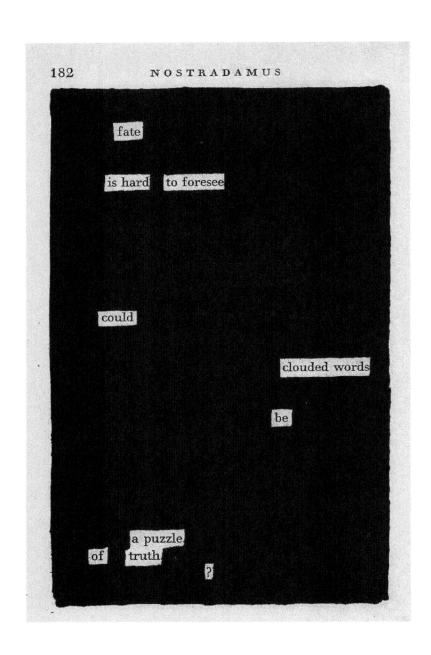

fate

is hard   to foresee

could

clouded words

be

a puzzle.
of   truth.
?

The Prophecies of Nostradamus

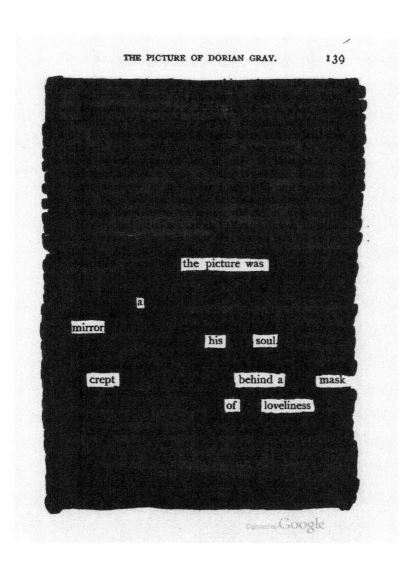

The Picture of Dorian Gray

Oscar Wilde

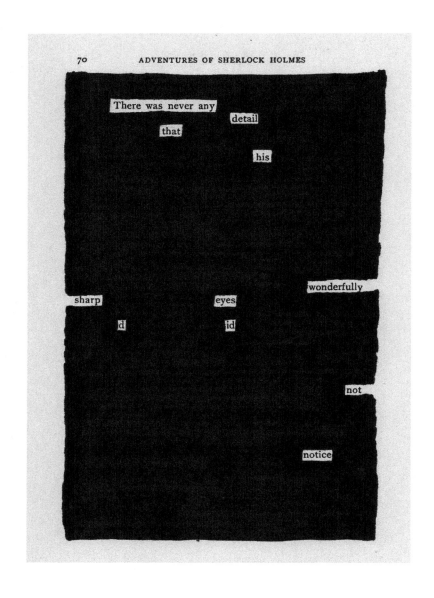

There was never any detail that his sharp eyes wonderfully d id not notice

The Adventures of Sherlock Holmes

Sir Arthur Conan Doyle

hope and

secrets of the Deep,

580

thy

soul

shalt possess

and.

590

deliverance
by the Woman's Seed
will be

600

the end.

Paradise (Not So) Lost

John Milton

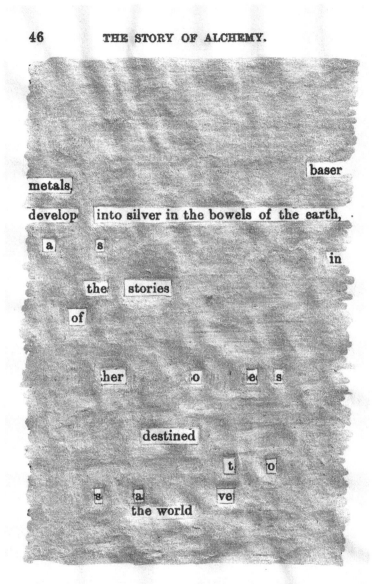

baser

metals,

develop into silver in the bowels of the earth,

a   s

in

the   stories

of

her   o   e   s

destined

t   o

s   a   ve

the world

The Hero(ine)'s Journey

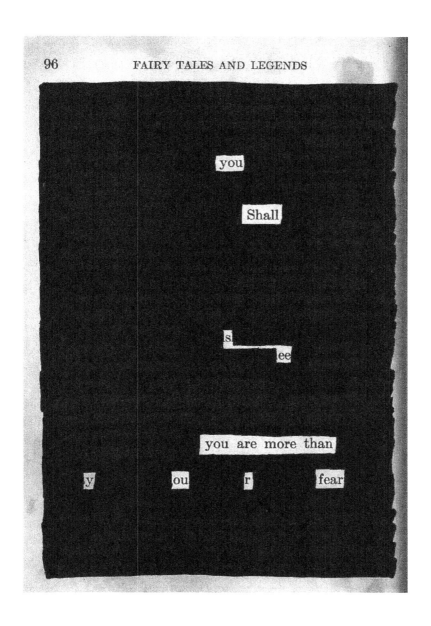

The Hero(ine)'s Lesson

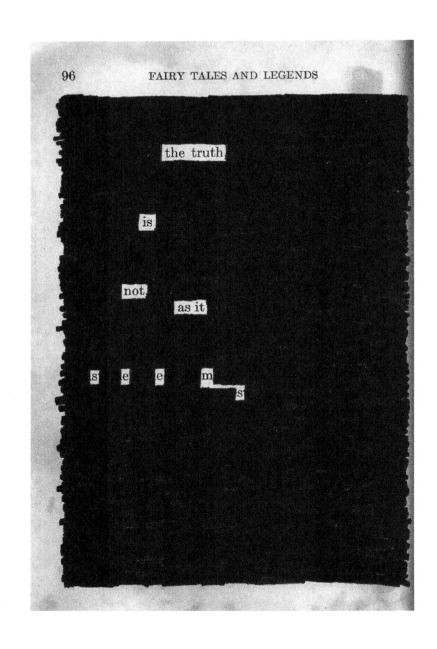

the truth

is

not,

as it

s e e m s

What We Learn from Fairy Tales

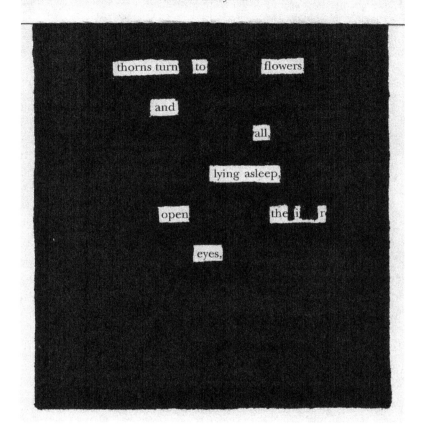

When the Curse Is Lifted

Part Three

true

life

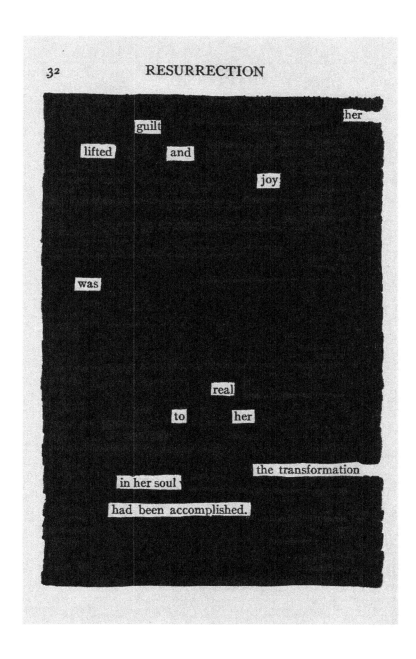

her
guilt
lifted   and
joy

was

real
to   her

the transformation
in her soul
had been accomplished.

Resurrection

CHAPTER III.

THE CHRYSALIS.

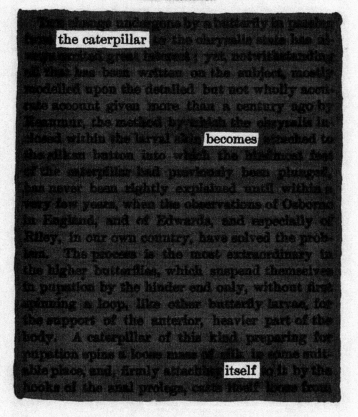

Metamorphosis

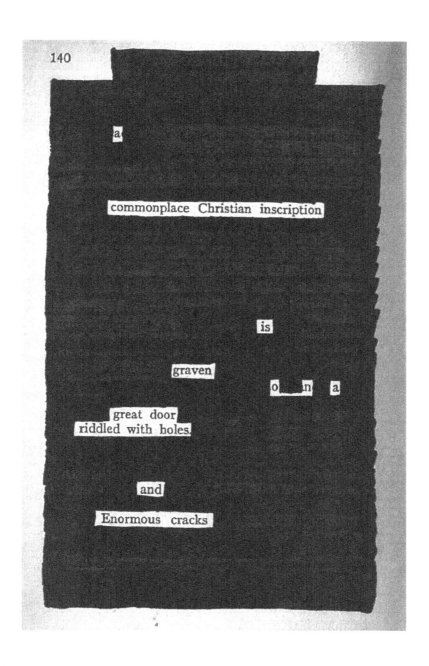

a

commonplace Christian inscription

is

graven

o   n   a

great door
riddled with holes

and

Enormous cracks

Hypocrisy

I

play the part

Well.

You're

intensely real.

Sincerity

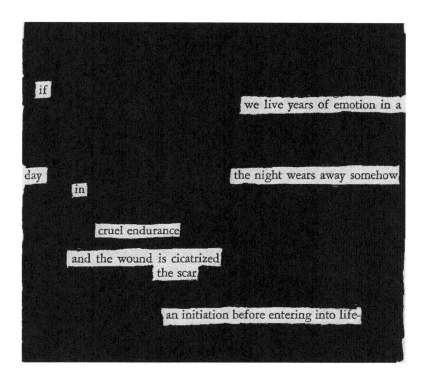

if

we live years of emotion in a

day

in

the night wears away somehow

cruel endurance

and the wound is cicatrized
the scar

an initiation before entering into life—

Years of Emotion

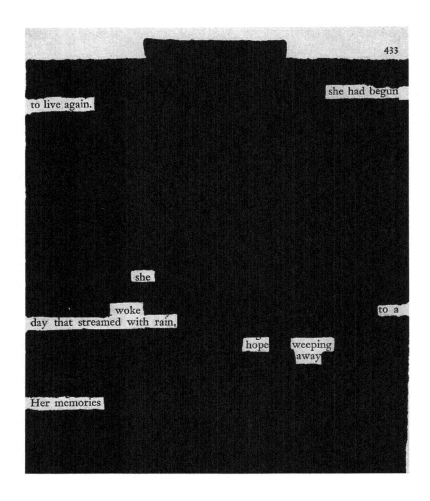

she had begun

to live again.

she

woke

day that streamed with rain,   to a

hope   weeping
away

Her memories

Hope Weeping

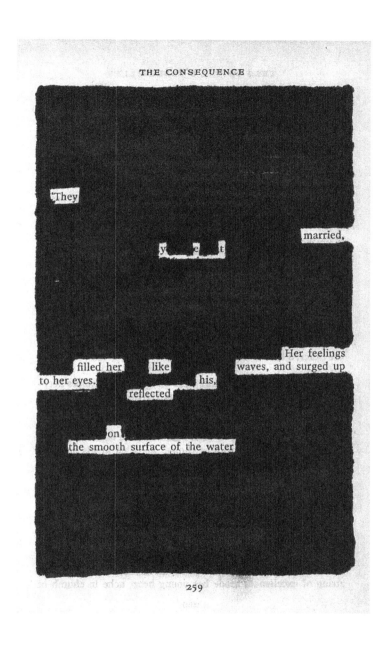

"They

married,

y e t

Her feelings
filled her   like   waves, and surged up
to her eyes.   his,
            reflected

            on
the smooth surface of the water

The Consequence

107

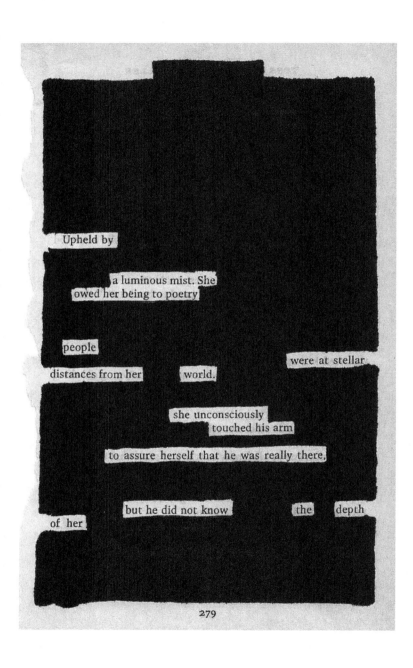

Upheld by

a luminous mist. She
owed her being to poetry

people

were at stellar

distances from her   world.

she unconsciously
touched his arm

to assure herself that he was really there,

but he did not know   the   depth

of her

279

The Depth of Her

108

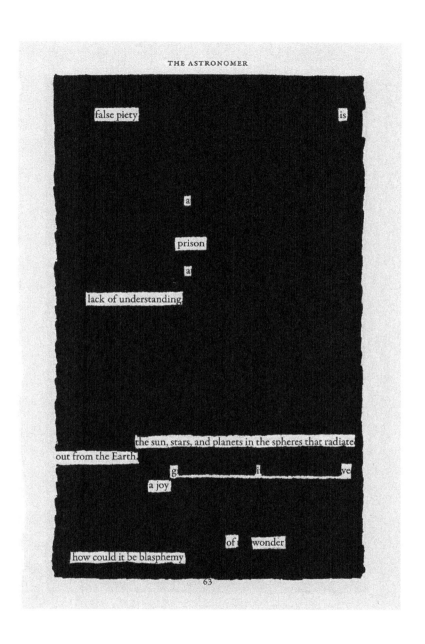

THE ASTRONOMER

false piety   is

a

prison

a

lack of understanding

the sun, stars, and planets in the spheres that radiate
out from the Earth.
                          g   i   ve
          a joy

                              of   wonder
how could it be blasphemy

63

The Astronomer's Advice, Part One

109

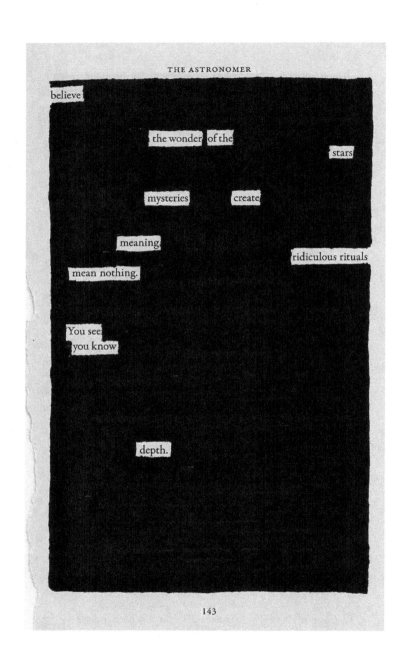

believe

the wonder of the

stars

mysteries   create

meaning,

ridiculous rituals

mean nothing.

You see,
you know

depth.

143

The Astronomer's Advice, Part Two

110

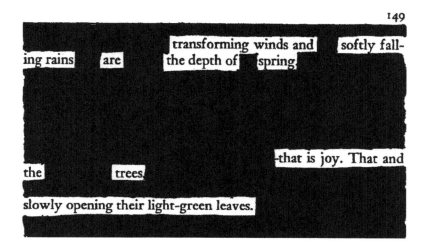

transforming winds and   softly fall-
ing rains   are   the depth of   spring.

—that is joy. That and
the   trees.
slowly opening their light-green leaves.

The Depth of Spring

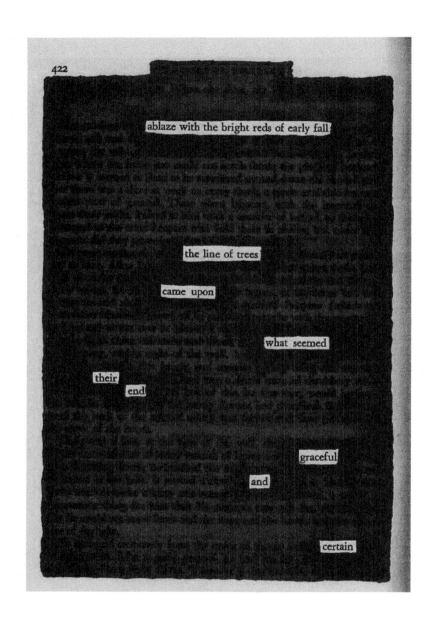

422

ablaze with the bright reds of early fall

the line of trees

came upon

what seemed

their
end

graceful

and

certain

Autumn

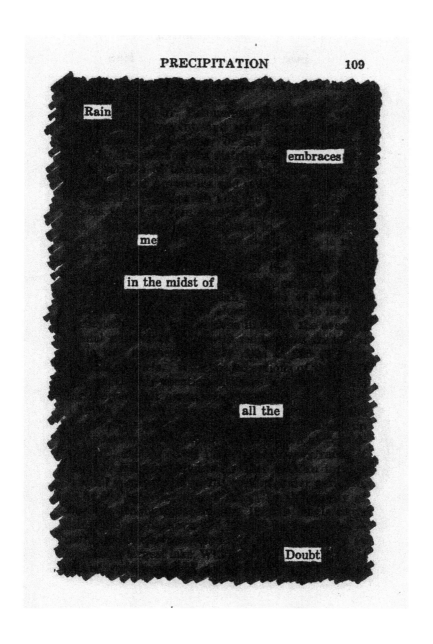

Rain Embraces Me

a continuous thunderstorm wi th lightning and tor-

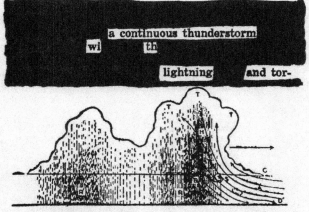

IDEAL CROSS SECTION OF A TYPICAL THUNDERSTORM

A, ascending air; *D*, descending air; *C*, storm collar; *D'*, wind gust; *H*, hail; *T*, thunderheads; *R*, primary rain; *R'*, secondary rain. (W. J. Humphreys.)

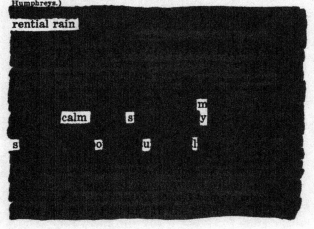

rential rain

calm s m y

s o u l

A Continuous Thunderstorm

114

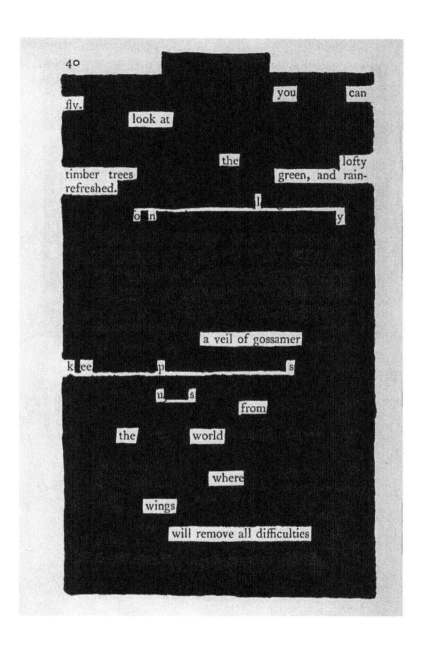

40

you   can
fly.
look at

the   lofty
timber trees   green, and rain-
refreshed.

only

a veil of gossamer

k ee   p   s

u   s

from

the   world

where

wings

will remove all difficulties

A Veil of Gossamer

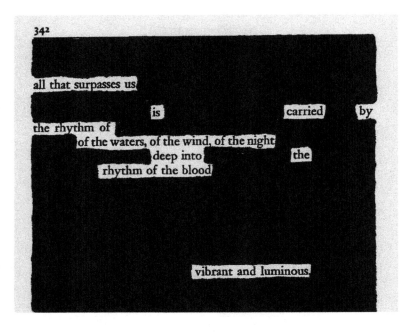

all that surpasses us

is   carried   by
the rhythm of
        of the waters, of the wind, of the night
                deep into   the
        rhythm of the blood

                        vibrant and luminous.

All That Surpasses Us

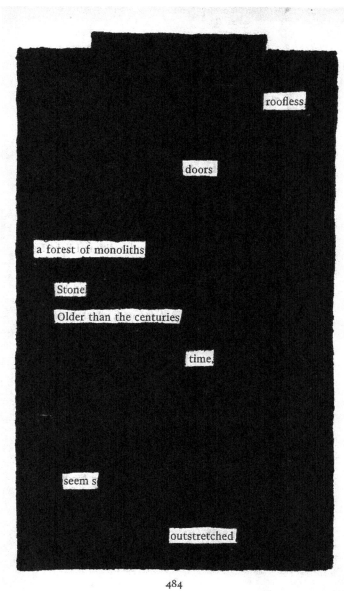

roofless.

doors

a forest of monoliths

Stone

Older than the centuries

time,

seem s

outstretched,

484

Stonehenge

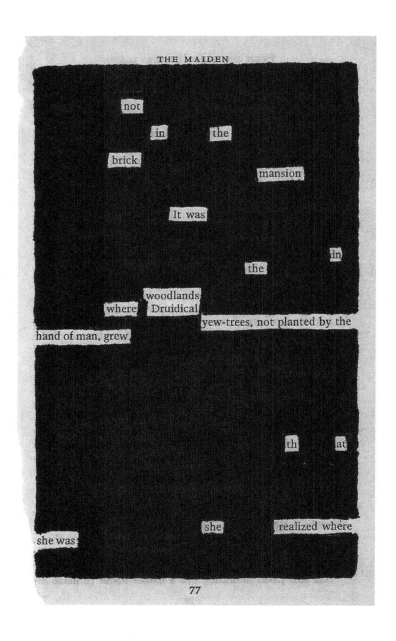

not

in   the

brick

mansion

It was

in

the

woodlands
where Druidical

yew-trees, not planted by the

hand of man, grew

th   at

she   realized where

she was

The Maiden

118

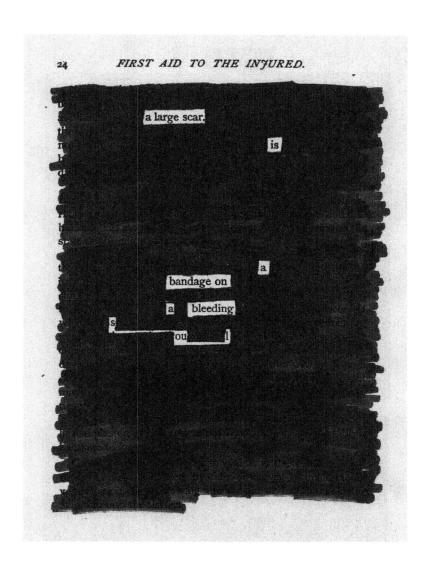

Bleeding Soul

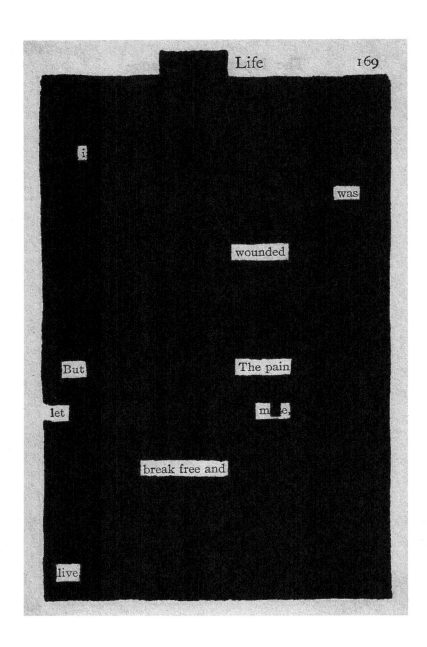

i

was

wounded

But

The pain

let

m e.

break free and

live.

Life

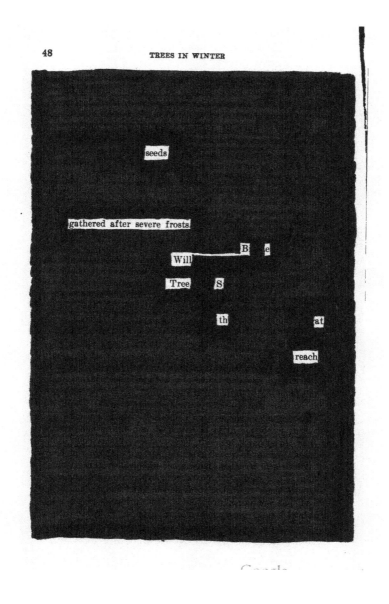

seeds

gathered after severe frosts.

B   e

Will

Tree   S

th   at

reach

Trees in Winter

life

still existed

but not in the shallows, only in the depths

Life Still Existed

Unaware

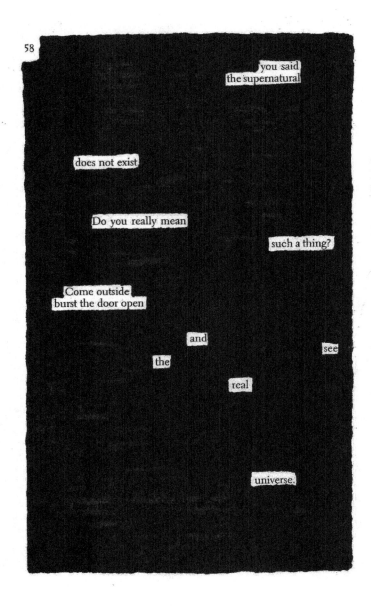

58

you said
the supernatural

does not exist.

Do you really mean

such a thing?

Come outside
burst the door open

and

see

the

real

universe.

The Real Universe

124

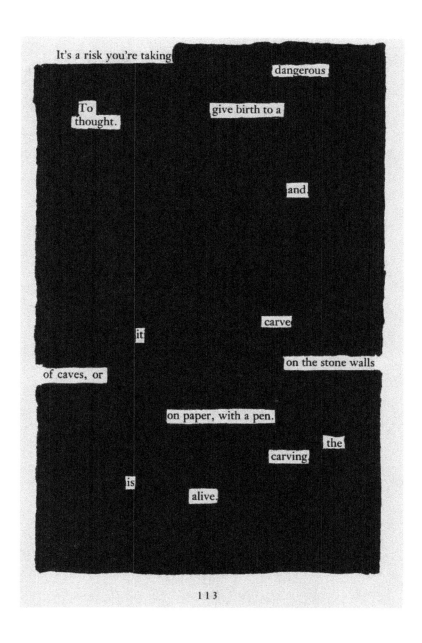

It's a risk you're taking

dangerous

To thought.

give birth to a

and

carve

it

on the stone walls

of caves, or

on paper, with a pen.

the

carving

is

alive.

The Courage to Write

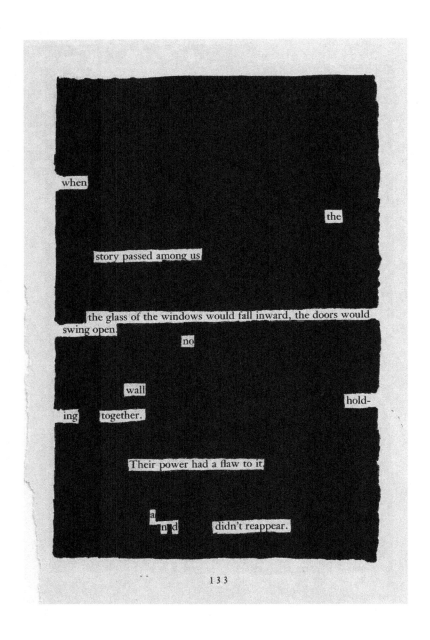

when

the

story passed among us

the glass of the windows would fall inward, the doors would swing open. no

wall

hold-

ing   together.

Their power had a flaw to it.

and   didn't reappear.

133

The Power of Story

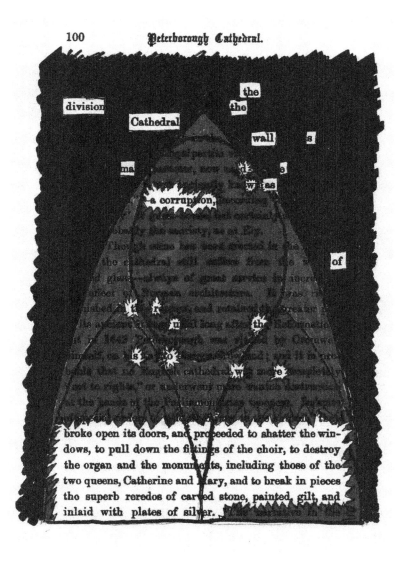

division the

the

Cathedral

wall s

a corruption,

of

broke open its doors, and proceeded to shatter the win-
dows, to pull down the fittings of the choir, to destroy
the organ and the monuments, including those of the
two queens, Catherine and Mary, and to break in pieces
the superb reredos of carved stone, painted, gilt, and
inlaid with plates of silver.

The Iconoclast's Defense

Rhetorical Whitewash

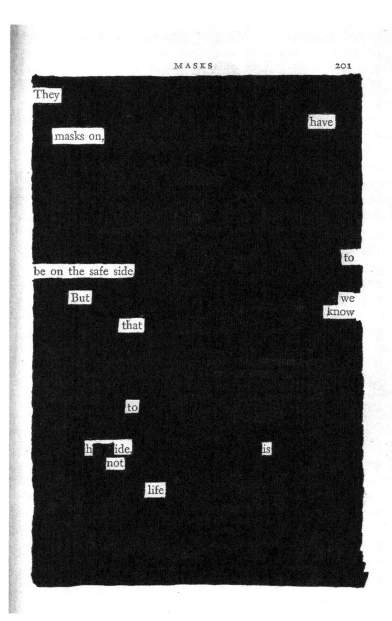

They have
masks on,

be on the safe side. to
But we
know
that

to

h ide. is
not.
life

Masks

129

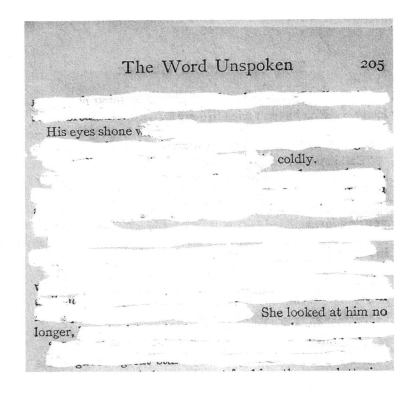

His eyes shone

coldly.

She looked at him no

longer,

The Word Unspoken

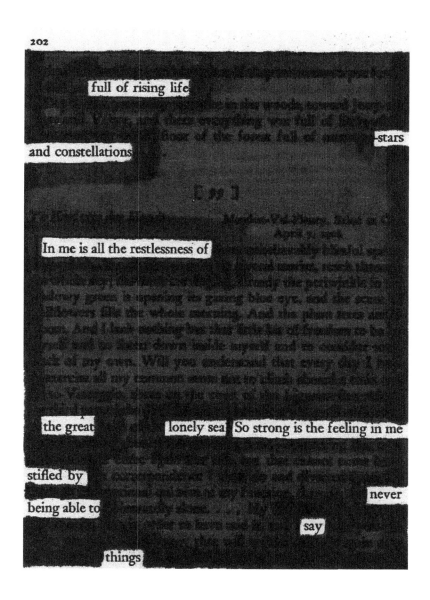

full of rising life

stars

and constellations

In me is all the restlessness of

the great lonely sea So strong is the feeling in me

stifled by

never

being able to

say

things

Writer's Block

131

lefdi is the Northern form of shortened *a* ... *lauedi* and *ladi* are Southern forms. The *a* was lengthened before cons. + vowels. *clay*—M.E. *ei* (A.S. *æg*) is generally represented in Modern English by the spellings *ai*, *ay*. M.E. *ēi*, A.S. *ēg*, *ēy* (Anglian *ēg*) has the same representation. These two M.E. diphthongs **suffered** shortening and followed the course of *ei*. Both short *e*'s were open in Middle English. M.E. *ei* (*ai*) passed to long open *e* through (*æi*) assimilated both elements to a long open *e*, and, after narrowing, passed to the diphthong (ei), which has now the first element open. There was a mixing of the spellings *ai* and *ei*. *neigh*—A.S. *ēg* has usually become (ai)—cp. *tie*, *dye* (page 252). *wave*—M.E. *wawe* is due to influence of *wawen* (A.S. *wagian* 'move'); *wave* has been influenced by the verb *wave* (A.S. *wafian*). *yea*—The **long** close *e* that was regularly got from M.E. *ę* was retained as in *break* and *great* (page 255). It has now become (ei) like the long close *e*'s that derived from M.E. *a*.

most—The long *o* is due to the *a* of the comparative (*mara mā*). A.S. *a* was rounded to *o* in Middle English. M.E. *ǭ* gives (ou). *cloth*—This **form** and pronunciation is due to the influence of *slaw* 'slow'. *loan*—*lān* and not *lēn* is responsible for this form. *moan*—due to influence of the noun *mone*, *moon* (?) (A.S. *mān* 'wickedness.')

(ii) is the regular development. *each*—For loss of *e* compare *which* and *such*. The *l* is retained in the North, e.g. Lowland Scotch *ilk*, which must not be confounded with another *ilk* **meaning** 'same' (A.S. *ylca*) *tease*—The form *toase* must be due to some form with A.S. *ā*. There is also a compound *to-tasen* 'to pull to pieces.' *taisen*—Perhaps the *i* is a parasite developed before a front consonant as in M.E.

The Purpose of Language

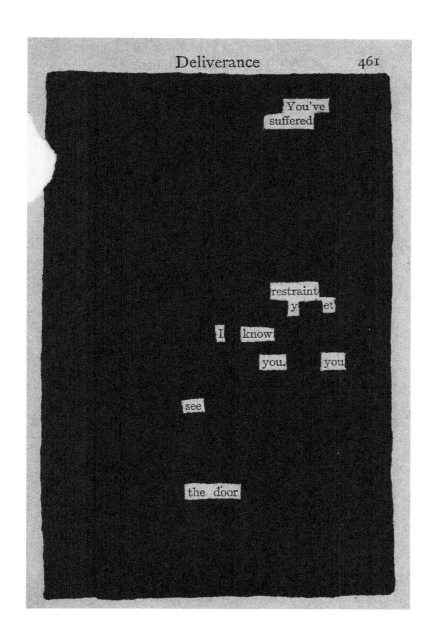

Deliverance

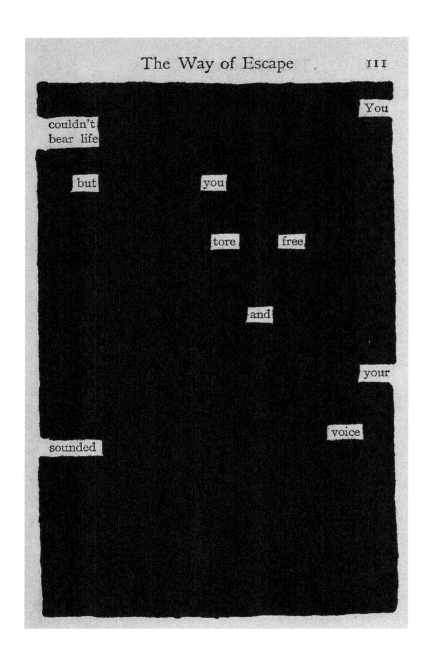

You

couldn't
bear life

but   you

tore   free

and

your

voice

sounded

The Way of Escape

134

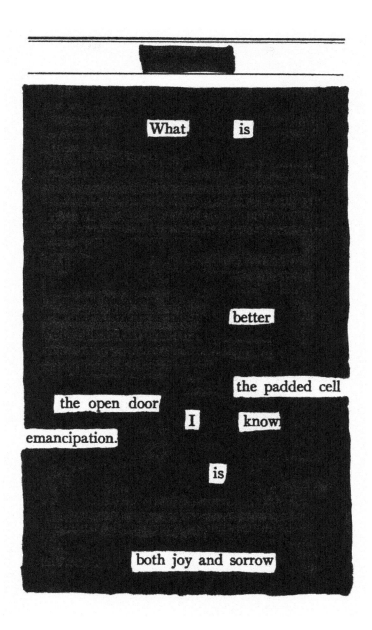

What is

better

the padded cell

the open door

I know

emancipation.

is

both joy and sorrow

Suburban Dilemma

135

your gypsying soul
Is caught and

Imprisoned

Your
longing   sighs.

Let your   soul float through
waves of the sea,

Its flight
steal over   walls—
to joy.

Your Gypsying Soul
from Rainer Maria Rilke

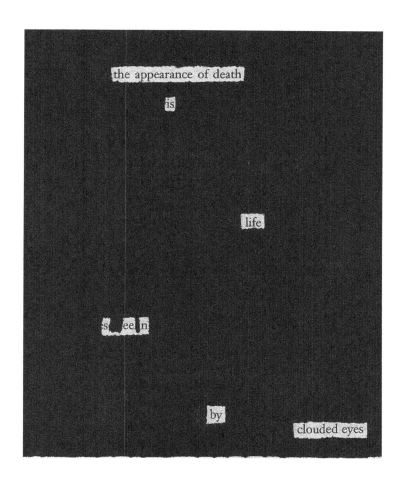

the appearance of death

is

life

s ee n

by

clouded eyes

The Appearance of Death

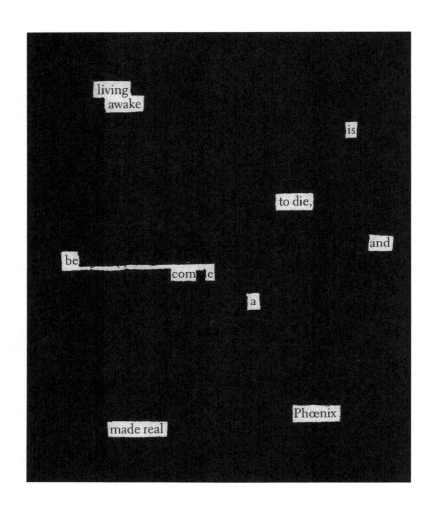

living
awake

is

to die,

and

be come

a

Phœnix

made real

Living Awake

138

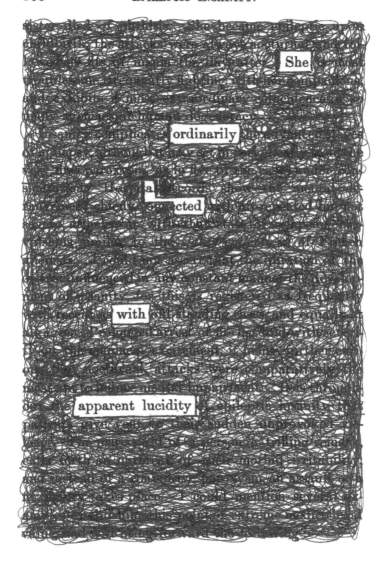

She

ordinarily

a
cted

with

apparent lucidity

Epileptic Insanity

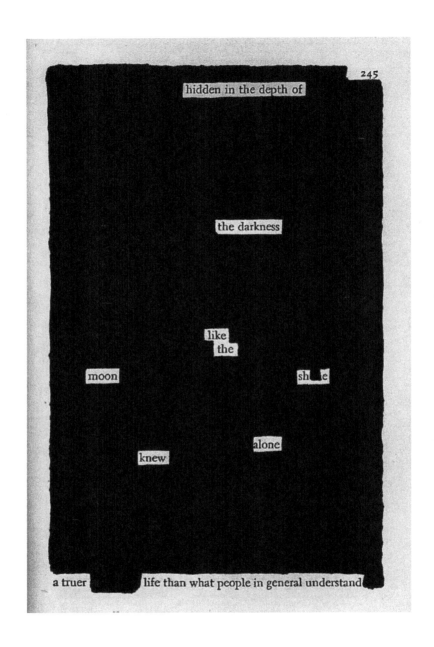

hidden in the depth of

the darkness

like
the

moon

sh__e

alone

knew

a truer life than what people in general understand

A Truer Life

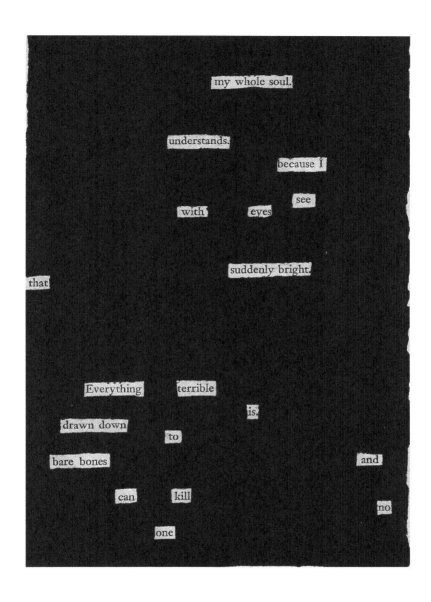

my whole soul.

understands.

because I

see

with eyes

suddenly bright.

that

Everything terrible

is

drawn down

to

bare bones and

can kill

no

one

Hope

words

are

mighty rivers

through pathless forests,

When

They

tell   the truth

Truthful Words

142

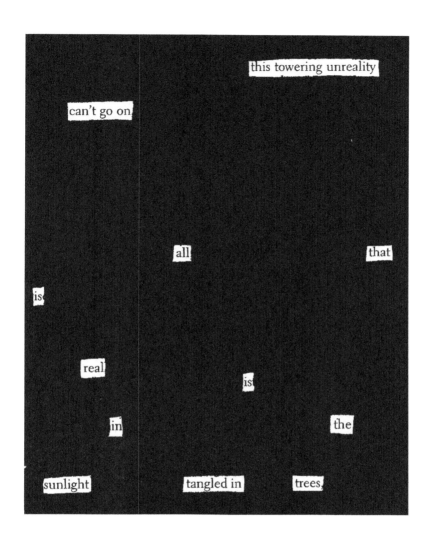

The Towering Unreality

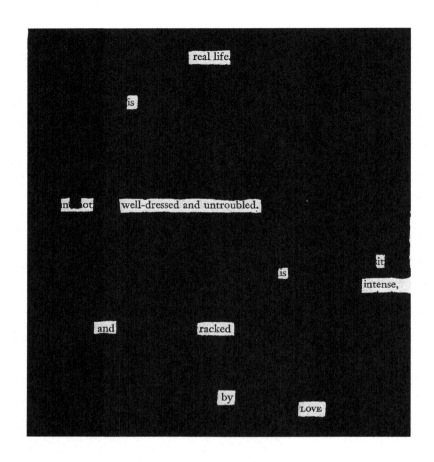

real life.

is

n[ ]ot   well-dressed and untroubled.

is   it

intense,

and   racked

by

LOVE

Real Life

Part Four

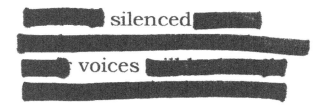

kingdome.   Let the sobbes therfore of thy prisoners, ô Lord, passe vp to thine eares, consider their affliction : and let the eyes of thy mercie looke downe vpon the blood of such as die for testimonie of thy eternal veritie ; and let not thine ennemies mocke thy iudgement for euer. To the, ô Lorde, I turne my wretched and wicked hart : to the alone I direct my complaint and grones : for in that Ile to thy saintes there is left no comfort. Albeit I haue thus (talkinge with my God in the anguishe of my harte) some what digressed : yet haue I not vtterlie forgotten my former proposition, to witt, that it is a thing repugnant to the ordre of nature, that any woman be exalted to rule ouer men. For God hath denied vnto her the office of a heade. And in the intreating of this parte, I remembre that I haue made the nobilitie both of England and Scotland inferior to brute beastes, for that they do to women which no male amongest the common sorte of beastes can be proued to do their females : that is, they reuerence them, and qwake at their presence, they obey their commandementes, and that against God. Wherfore I iudge them not onelie subiectes to women, but sclaues of Satan, and seruantes of iniquitie. If any man thinke these my wordes sharpe or vehement, let him consider that the offense is more haynous, than can be expressed by wordes. For where all thinges, be expressedly concluded against the glorie and honor of God, and where the blood of the saintes of God is commanded to be shed, whome shall we iudge, God or the deuil, to be presi-
NOTE   dent of that counsel ?   Plain it is, that God ruleth not by his loue, mercie, nor grace in the assembly of the vngodlie. Then it resteth, that the deuil, the prince of this worlde, doth reigne ouer suche tyrannes. whose seruantes, I pray you, shal then be iudged, such as obey, and execute their tyrannie ? God for his great mercies sake, illuminate the eyes of men, that they may perceiue in to what miserable bondage they be broght, by the monstriferous empire of women.

The seconde glasse, whiche God hath set before the eyes of
NOTE   man, wherein he may beholde the ordre, whiche pleaseth his wisdome, concerning authoritie and dominion, is that common welth, to the whiche it pleaseth his maiestie to apoint, and geue lawes, statutes, rites and ceremonies not onelie concerninge religion, but also touching their policie and

The Secret Revisions of Mistress Margaret Knox

149

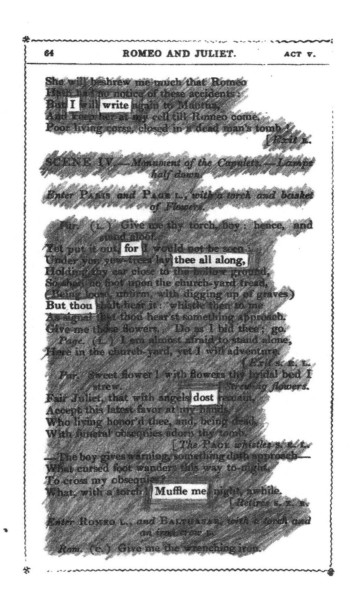

She will beshrew me much that Romeo
Hath had no notice of these accidents;
But I will **write** again to Mantua,
And keep her at my cell till Romeo come;
Poor living corse, closed in a dead man's tomb !
                          [*Exit* r.

SCENE IV.—*Monument of the Capulets.*—*Lamps
half down.*

Enter PARIS *and* PAGE L., *with a torch and basket
of Flowers.*

Par. (L.) Give me thy torch, boy : hence, and
         stand aloof.
Yet put it out : **for** I would not be seen ;
Under yon yew-trees lay **thee all along,**
Holding thy ear close to the hollow ground,
So shall no foot upon the church-yard tread,
(Being loose, unfirm, with digging up of graves)
But thou shalt hear it : whistle then to me
As signal that thou hear'st something approach.
Give me those flowers. Do as I bid thee ; go.
    Page. (L.) I am almost afraid to stand alone,
Here in the church-yard, yet I will adventure.
                         [*Exit* s. e. l.
    Par. Sweet flower ! with flowers thy bridal bed I
         strew.   *Strewing flowers.*
Fair Juliet, that with angels **dost** remain,
Accept this latest favor at my hands,
Who living honor'd thee, and, being dead,
With funeral obsequies adorn thy tomb.
             [*The* PAGE *whistles* s. e. l.
— The boy gives warning, something doth approach—
What cursed foot wanders this way to-night,
To cross my obsequies ?
What, with a torch ! **Muffle me,** night, awhile.
                      [*Retires* s. e. r.

Enter ROMEO L., *and* BALTHASAR, *with a torch and
an iron crow.*

Rom. (L.) Give me the wrenching iron.

The Secret Revisions of Mistress Anne Shakespeare

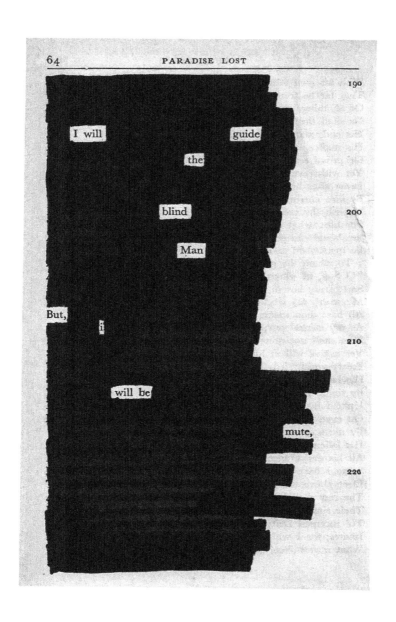

The Secret Revisions of Mistress Mary Milton upon Her Father's Epic

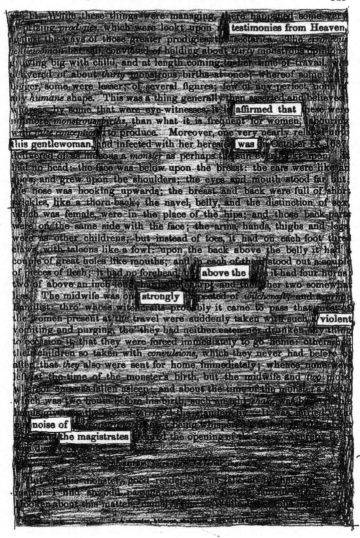

The Secret Revisions of Mistress Abigail Mather upon Her Husband's Ecclesiastical History of New England

many foule and fundamentall errors, and after be cast out for notorious lying.

5. That shee who was wont to bee so confident of her spirituall good estate, and ready (undesired) to hold it forth to others (being pressed now at her last appearance before the Church to give some proofs of it) should bee wholly silent in that matter.

6. Whereas upon the sentence of the Court against her, shee boasted highly of her sufferings for Christ, &c. it was noted by one of the Elders (who bare witnesse against her errors) that the spirit of glory promised in 1 Pet. to those who suffer for well-doing, did not come upon her, but a spirit of delusion, and damnable error, which, as it had possessed her before, so it became more effectuall and evident by her sufferings.

7. Here is to bee seen the presence of God in his Ordinances, when they are faithfully attended according to his holy will, although not free from human infirmities. This American Jesabel kept her strength and reputation, even among the people of God, till the hand of Civill Justice laid hold on her, and then shee began evidently to decline, and the faithfull to bee freed from her forgeries; and now in this last act, when shee might have expected (as most likely shee did) by her seeming repentance of her errors, and confessing her undervaluing of the Ordinances of Magistracy and Ministery, to have redeemed her reputation in point of sincerity, and yet have made good all her former work, and kept open a back doore to have returned to her vomit again, by her paraphrasticall retractions, and denying any change in her judgement, yet such was the presence and blessing of God in his owne Ordinance, that this subtilty of Satan was discovered to her utter shame and confusion, and to the setting at liberty of many godly hearts, that had been captivated by her to that day, and that Church which by her means was brought

¹ 1 Peter, iii. 17; iv. 14.

The Secret Revisions of Mistress Elizabeth Winthrop upon Her Husband's Account of the Trial of Mistress Anne Hutchinson

Huswifery

BY EDWARD TAYLOR

Make me, O Lord,

in t o thy Swift Flyer

n o t

in

t o

a Web

O F

y

arn

The Secret Revisions of Mistress Elizabeth Fitch Taylor upon Her Husband's Poem

sinners up from perdition, as one holds a loathsome
  over the glowing embers, is angry with them, is
fearfully provoked, his anger burns like fire. He views
you as fit for nothing else but to suffer an hour of his
law. He is of purer eyes than to bear you long in his
sight. He sees no such deformity elsewhere as he sees
in you, not even in the most loathsome serpent. No
rebel ever offended his prince as you have offended God
and still his own kind hand holds you back from the
doom you deserve. To nothing else can it be ascribed
that you went not to the place of torment the last night,
that you waked from sleep this morning, that you have
not perished since you waked, and that you do not this
moment quit us to go to the world of misery. The
iniquities of your hearts, while you sit here under the
sound of the gospel rejecting a Saviour, constantly tempt
him to abandon you forever.

O sinner! consider the danger you are in. The per-
dition that yawns beneath you is wide and bottomless,
and the God who holds you up from it is fearfully in-
censed against you, even as he is against those who have
gone to suffer their doom. The moment will come, and
may while I am speaking, that shall see the thread sun-
dered that sustains you. And you no interest in a Medi-
ator, no hiding place, nothing to lay hold of to prevent
your fall, nothing to appease the divine indignation,
nothing that you have done, nothing that you *are doing*,
nothing that you *can do*. Your whole interest is at
hazard, and your soul at hazard.

Let me suggest four thoughts respecting the wrath you
are in danger of, and I have done.

1. Whose wrath it is. *It is the wrath of the infinite
God.* Were it merely the wrath of man, though of the
most powerful prince, it would be comparatively nothing.

The Secret Revisions of Mrs. Sarah Edwards

his

arduous pro-

ject of arriving at moral perfection.

was not sufficient

The Secret Revisions of Mrs. Deborah Franklin

of the amendment, however, were agreed on, that is to say, the freedom of all born after a certain day, and deportation at a proper age. But it was found that the public mind would not yet bear the proposition, nor will it bear it even at this day. Yet the day is not distant when it must bear and adopt it, or worse will follow. Nothing is more certainly written in the book of fate, than that these people are to be free; nor is it less certain that the two races, equally free, cannot live in the same government. Nature, habit, opinion have drawn indelible lines of distinction between them. It is still in our power to direct the process of emancipation and deportation, peaceably, and in such slow degree, as that the evil will wear off insensibly, and their place be, pari passu, filled up by free white laborers. If, on the contrary, it is left to force itself on, human nature must shudder at the prospect held up. We should in vain look for an example in the Spanish deportation or deletion of the Moors. This precedent would fall far short of our case.

I considered four of these bills, passed or reported, as forming a system by which every fibre would be eradicated of ancient or future aristocracy; and a foundation laid for a government truly republican. The repeal of the laws of entail would prevent the accumulation and perpetuation of wealth, in select families, and preserve the soil of the country from being daily more and more absorbed in mortmain. The abolition of primogeniture, and equal partition of inheritances, removed the feudal and unnatural distinctions which made one member of every family rich, and all the rest poor, substituting equal partition, the best of all Agrarian laws. The restoration of the rights of conscience relieved the people from taxation for the support of a religion not theirs; for the establishment was truly of the religion of the rich, the dissenting sects being entirely composed of the less wealthy people; and these, by the bill for a general education, would be qualified to understand their rights, to maintain them, and to exercise with intelligence their parts in self-government; and all this would be effected, without the violation of a single natural right of any one individual citizen. To these, too, might be add-

The Secret Revisions of Sally Hemings upon her Master Thomas Jefferson's Autobiography

is

his song

30

;

poetical,

and

40

always full of love

his

soul

is

not

50

The Secret Revisions of Mrs. Sara Coleridge

(the delivery of the money, and murder committed within three days upon the party receiving it) happen to all of us every hour of our lives without attracting even momentary notice. Coincidences, in general, are great stumbling-blocks in the way of that class of thinkers who have been educated to know nothing of the theory of probabilities—that theory to which the most glorious objects of human research are indebted for the most glorious of illustration. In the present instance, had the gold been gone, the fact of its delivery three days before would have formed something more than a coincidence. It would have been corroborative of this idea of motive. But, under the real circumstances of the case, if we are to suppose gold the motive of this outrage, we must also imagine the perpetrator so vacillating an idiot as to have abandoned his gold and his motive together.

"Keeping now steadily in mind the points to which I have drawn your attention—that peculiar voice, that unusual agility, and that startling absence of motive in a murder so singularly atrocious as this—let us glance at the butchery itself. Here is a woman strangled to death by manual strength, and thrust up a chimney, head downward. Ordinary assassins employ no such modes of murder as this. Least of all do they thus dispose of the murdered. In the manner of thrusting the corpse up the chimney, you will admit that there was something *excessively outré*—something altogether irreconcilable with our common notions of human action, even when we suppose the actors the most depraved of men. Think, too, how great must have been that strength which could have thrust the body *up* such an aperture so forcibly that the united vigor of several persons was found barely sufficient to drag it *down!*

"Turn, now, to other indications of the employment

The Secret Revisions of Mrs. Virginia Poe

truth

h   s

m   orie

power

th   an

fact   wh   e   n

hope

possesses wings

The Secret Revisions of Mrs. Emma Darwin

treme of reserve. But the contrary extreme, of manifesting an excessive fondness for the society of gentlemen, is still more to be avoided. By cultivating an acute sense of propriety in all things, with a nice discrimination of judgment, you will be able generally to direct your conduct aright in these matters.

Never indulge feelings of partiality for any man until he has distinctly avowed his own sentiments, and you have deliberately determined the several points already mentioned. If you do, you may subject yourself to much needless disquietude, and perhaps the most unpleasant disappointments. And the wounded feeling thus produced may have an injurious effect upon your subsequent character and happiness.

I shall close this chapter with a few brief remarks, of a general nature :

1. Do not suffer this subject to occupy a very prominent place in your thoughts. To be constantly ruminating upon it, can hardly fail of exerting an injurious influence upon your mind, feelings, and deportment ; and you will be almost certain to betray yourself in the society of gentlemen, and, perhaps, become the subject of merriment, as one who is anxious for a husband

2. Do not make this a subject of common conversation. There is, perhaps, nothing which has a stronger tendency to deteriorate the social intercourse of young people, than the disposition to give

The Secret Revisions of the Students of the Clergy Daughters' School, Part One

having been hitherto chiefly addressed to the male sex. They are now sedulously laboring to destroy the religious principles of women, and in too many instances have fatally succeeded. For this purpose, novels and romances have been made the vehicles of vice and infidelity."

6. *Novel reading is a great waste of time.* Few will pretend that they read novels with any higher end in view than *mere amusement*; while, by the strong excitement they produce, they impose a heavier tax on both mind and body than any other species of mental effort. If any thing valuable is to be derived from them, it may be obtained with far less expense of time, and with safety to the morals, from other sources. No Christian, who feels the obligation of "redeeming the time because the days are evil," will fail to feel the force of this remark. We have no more right to squander our time, and waste our energies in frivolous pursuits, than we have to waste our money in extravagant expenditures. We are as much the *stewards* of God in respect to the one as the other.

7. *Novel reading is a great hinderance to serious piety.* Such is the mental intoxication produced by it, that we might as well attempt to reach the conscience of the inebriate, with the truths of God's word, as that of the novel reader; and the heart that can be feasted on such dainties cannot have sufficient relish for the "sincere milk of the word" to "grow thereby." The following testi-

13

The Secret Revisions of the Students at the Clergy Daughters' School, Part Two

be a Negro also, brown skin, kinky hair and all. It is a matter of education, morality and money; and just as soon as the majority of negroes acquire these, the question of color will begin to drop out. Are you doing what you can to hasten that day?" The idea among all classes of negroes — teachers and pupils — is monstrously wrong. For the most part they seek only to be like the whites rather than to obtain the qualities which make the white man superior. The question of color will not drop out. On the other hand, the Negro is encouraged in imitating the white man and then abused because he does it; we expect him to imitate the good in the stronger race and not the bad. We give the white children lessons which we desire to be incentives to learning, culture, and high ideals; when the Negro reads the same lessons, if he should aspire to the same ideals, he is accused of being criminal. Perhaps he can not aspire; he imitates.

The suggestion made here is that the text books of the first years for the negroes should be very different from those of the white children. It is hoped that the suggestion will merit serious consideration and to this end brief explanation is given. No outline of the proposed books will be given here but the general plan may be indicated. New text books are desirable for two main reasons. First, books are needed which are especially suited to the negroes as a race, to develop the negro child *within his race*. The second may be stated more fully: Text books are needed which are especially adapted to the negro *mind*, texts based on the most accurate and sympathetic knowledge of the characteristics of the Negro, which comprehend the peculiar needs of negro children, which are carefully planned and graded to teach the things fundamental in their proper education. It is essential that details be taught from the very beginning, and by constant drill the habit of doing

The Secret Revisions of the Students of the Tuskegee Institute

not excited by sensory stimuli . . . but it is not the lack of sensory stimuli that conditions sleep, but rather a lack of interest for the same; some sensory impressions are even necessary in so far as they serve to calm the mind; thus the miller can fall asleep only when he hears the rattling of his mill, and he who finds it necessary to burn a light at night, as a matter of precaution, cannot fall asleep in the dark " (p. 457).

"The psyche isolates itself during sleep from the outer world, and withdraws from the periphery. . . . Nevertheless, the connection is not entirely interrupted; if one did not hear and feel even during sleep, but only after awakening, he would certainly never awake. The continuance of sensation is even more plainly shown by the fact that we are not always awakened by the mere sensory force of the impression, but by the psychic relation of the same; an indifferent word does not arouse the sleeper, but if called by name he awakens . . . hence the psyche differentiates sensations during sleep. It is for this reason that we may be awakened by the lack of a sensory stimulus if it relates to the presentation of an important thing; thus one awakens when the light is extinguished, and the miller when the mill comes to a standstill; that is, the awakening is due to the cessation of a sensory activity, which presupposes that it has been perceived, and that it has not disturbed the mind, being indifferent or rather gratifying " (p. 460, &c.).

"If we are willing to disregard these objections, which are not to be taken lightly, we still must admit that the qualities of the dream-life thus far considered, which originate by withdrawing from the outer world, cannot fully explain the strangeness of the dream. For otherwise it would be possible to change back the hallucinations of the dream into presentations and the situations of the dream into thoughts, and thus to perform the task of dream interpretation. Now this is what we do when we reproduce the dream from memory after awakening, and whether we are fully or only partially successful in this back translation the dream still retains its mysteriousness undiminished.

Furthermore all the authors assume unhesitatingly that still other more far-reaching alterations take place in the presentation material of waking life. One of them, Strümpell,[44]

The Secret Revisions of Frau Anna Freud

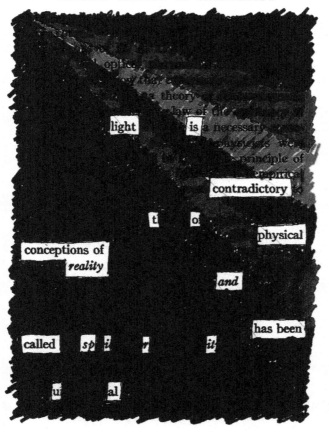

light   is a necessary

principle of

contradictory

physical

conceptions of
reality

and

has been

called   sp i r   it

u   al

The Secret Revisions of Mrs. Elsa Einstein

Chapter 13

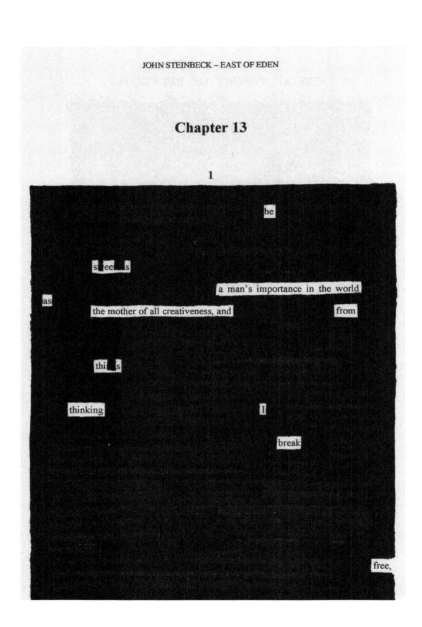

The Secret Revisions of Mrs. Carol Steinbeck

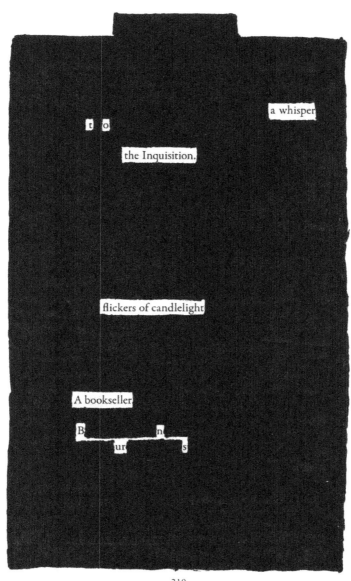

t o   a whisper

the Inquisition,

flickers of candlelight

A bookseller.

B   n
   ur   s

210

Censorship

167

a Degree of Blindness,

as ancient as human Nature,

A Degree of Blindness

19

C H A P. III.

Whether Women *are equal to* Men *in their Intellectual Capacity, or not.*

IF the Business of the Mind were nothing more than to contrive a Dress; to invent a new Fashion; to set off a bad Face; to heighten the Charms of a good one; to understand the Œconomy of a Tea-table; to manage an Intrigue; to conduct a Game at *Quadrille*; and to lay out new Plans of Pleasure, Pride, and Luxury: the *Women* must be owned to have a Capacity not only *equal*, but even superior to us. But, as the Understanding of *Man* has infinitely higher Objects to employ its Speculations on, Objects beyond the very Aim of the ablest of *Women*; their intellectual Faculties are so evidently inferior to his, that I should think it an Impertinence in me to take up any Time to prove it, if my fair Adversary was not *Woman* enough to call so palpable a Truth in Question.

Need we look any farther than their soft, simpering, silly Faces, to fathom the perceptible Depth of their Understandings? View the whole Sex round:

Eternal Smiles their Emptiness betray,
As shallow Streams run dimpling all the Way. Pope.

A thoughtless Stare, a wild Vivacity, a sleepy Pertness, giddy Gravity, or some such other Sense-defying Look, betray, in *all*, the narrow Space between the Surface and the Centre of their mimic Wit. How well the masterly Limner knew them, who snatched from them the Graces he so skilfully bestowed on *Sporus*, that Copy of themselves, in-

D 2   spired

The Voice of Everywoman

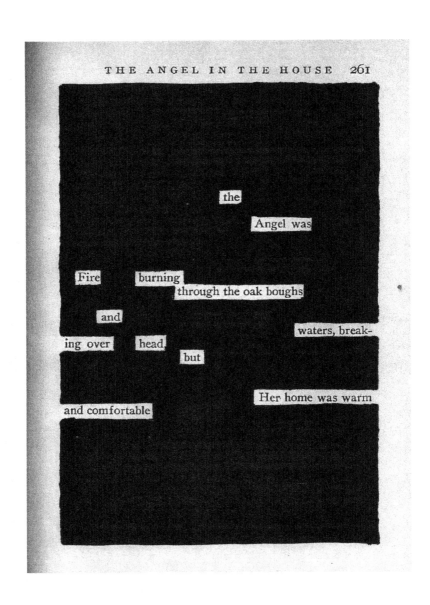

The Angel in the House

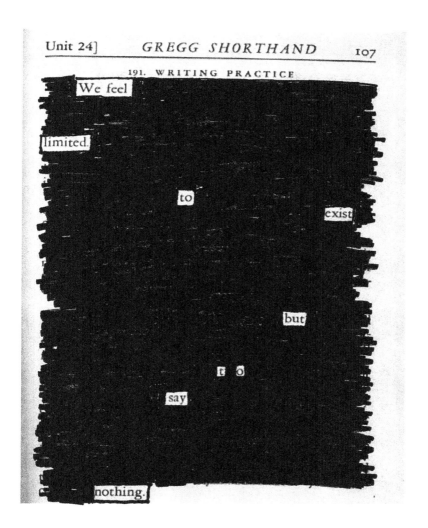

191. WRITING PRACTICE

We feel

limited.

to

exist

but

t o

say

nothing.

The Stenographer's Complaint

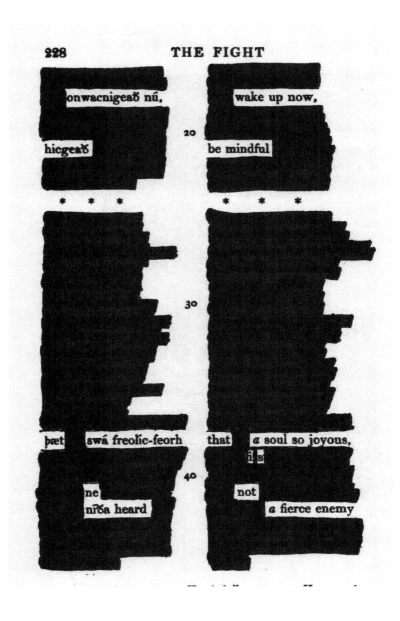

onwacnigeað nú,   wake up now,

20

hicgeað   be mindful

*   *   *   *   *   *

30

þæt   swá freolíc-feorh   that   *a* soul so joyous,

40

ne   not
nǐða heard   *a* fierce enemy

The Peace-weaver's Advice

Part Five

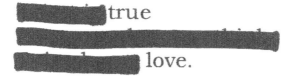

████████ true
████████████████████████
████████████ love.

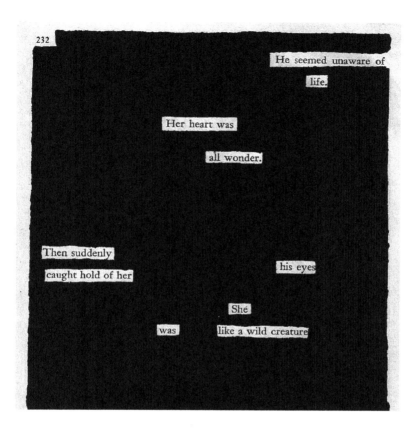

He seemed unaware of
life.

Her heart was

all wonder.

Then suddenly
caught hold of her
his eyes

She
was like a wild creature

Connection

he had seen her

she raised her eyes,

she had never

been

seen

before

Being Seen

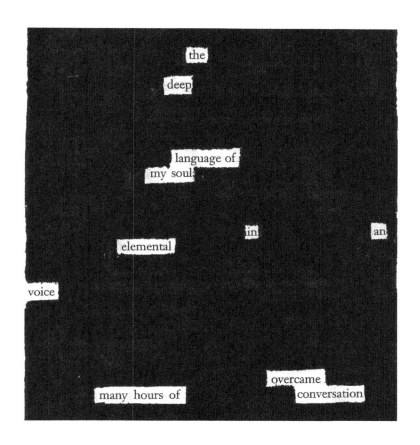

the

deep

language of
my soul:

in   an

elemental

voice

overcame
many hours of   conversation

The Language of My Soul

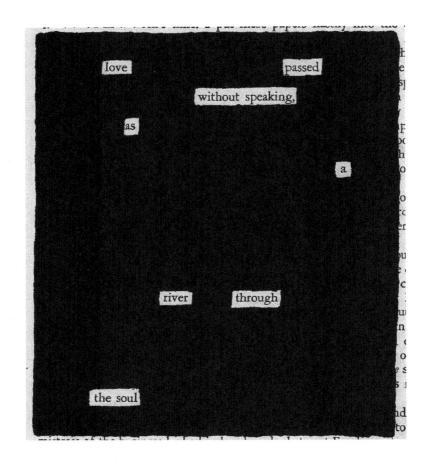

A River Through the Soul

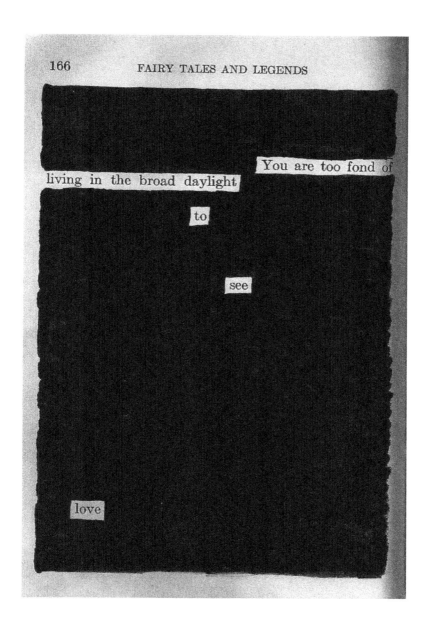

living in the broad daylight You are too fond of to see love

To See Love

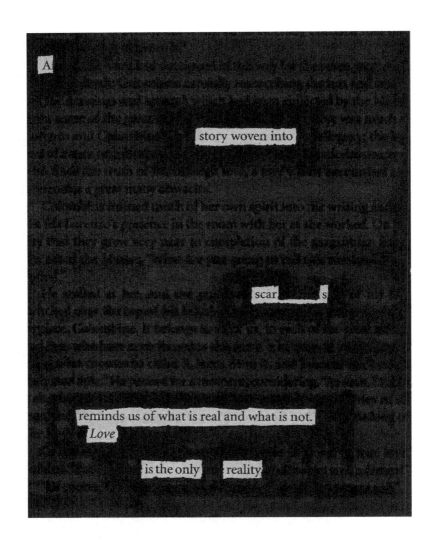

A story woven into scar_____s reminds us of what is real and what is not. Love is the only reality.

A Story Woven into Scars

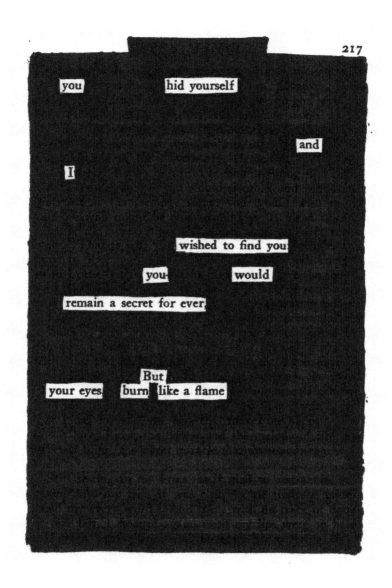

you   hid yourself

and

I

wished to find you

you-   would

remain a secret for ever.

But
your eyes, burn like a flame

Finding You

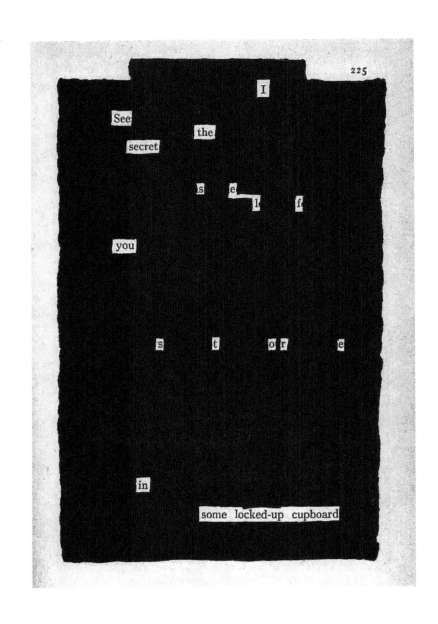

I

See

the

secret

s e
l

f

you

s t o r e

in

some locked-up cupboard

Secret Self

THE CIRCULATION.

of

his

blood is effected by

her

heart.

Lifeblood

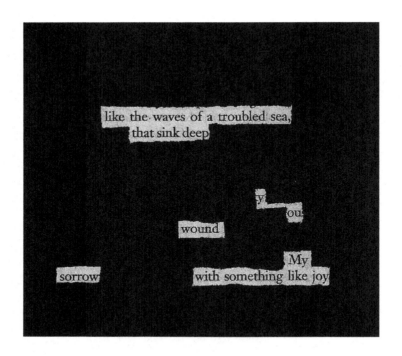

like the waves of a troubled sea,
that sink deep

y
ou

wound

My

sorrow   with something like joy

You Wound My Sorrow

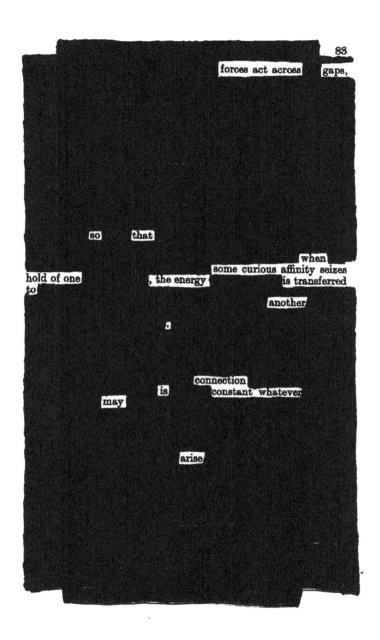

forces act across gaps,

so that

when some curious affinity seizes
hold of one , the energy is transferred
to another

connection
is constant whatever
may

arise

Synchronicity of Souls

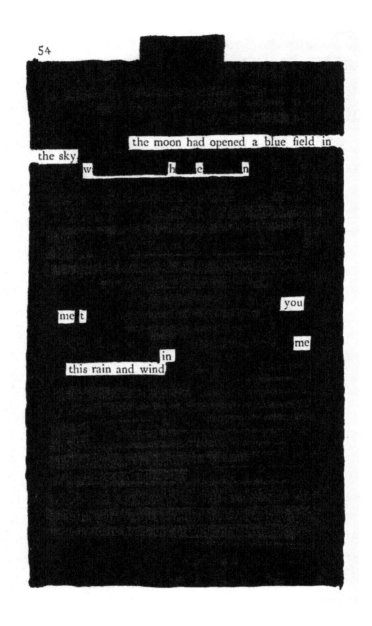

54

the moon had opened a blue field in
the sky. w h e n

me t   you

                                    me

                    in
this rain and wind

You Met Me

188

CHAPTER VII

THE

moon was rising
deep and mysterious
across her path.

They saw each other

At last

on such a night as this

Such a Night as This

THE WOMAN WHO LOVES

██████████████████. To you I glide

████████████████████████████████████
██████████████████████████████████████
███████████ as

████ unfaltering and swift and strong ██

██
███████████████████████████████████
██████████████████████████ waters flow.

██
Something within me has been freed— ████████

████████████████████████████████████
Which rises now within me ██████████████

██
██

The Woman Who Loves
from Rainer Maria Rilke

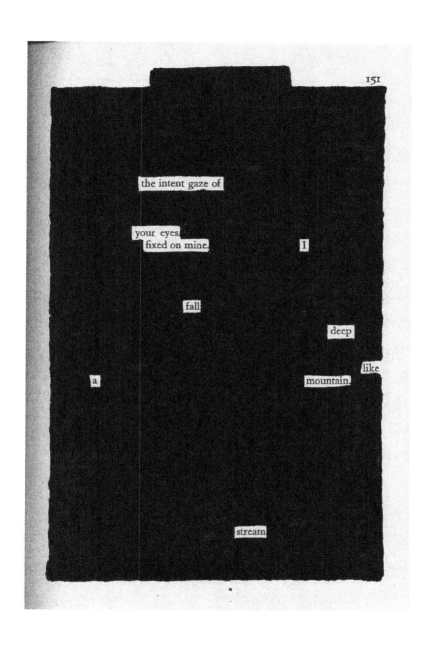

I Fall Deep

191

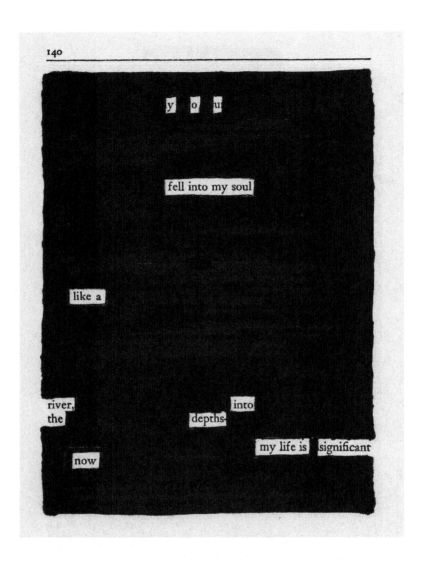

You Fell into My Soul

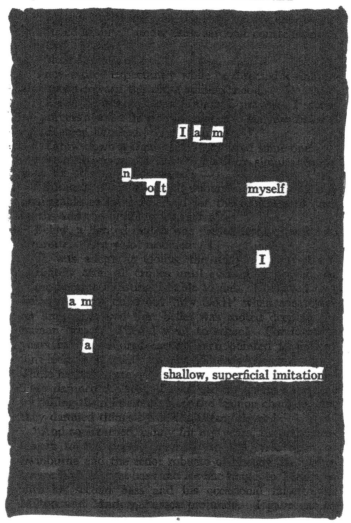

Not Myself

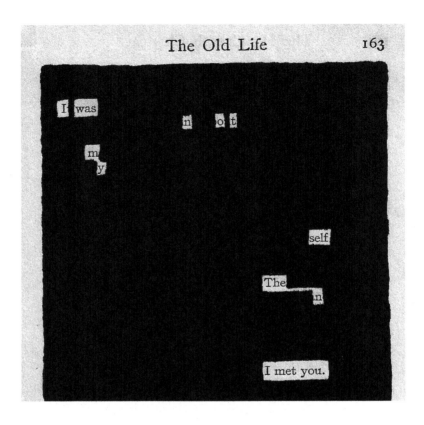

I was n o t m y self. The n I met you.

Then I Met You

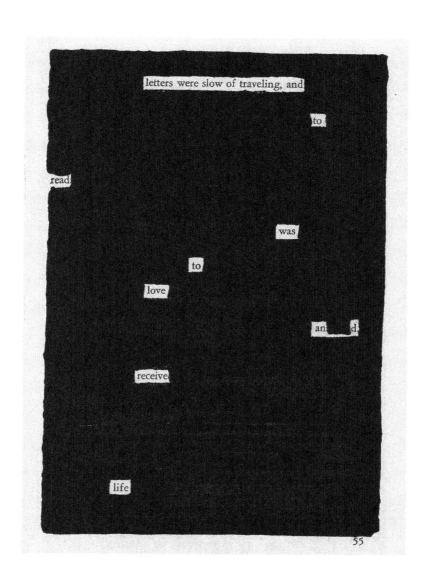

letters were slow of traveling, and
to
read
was
to
love
an d.
receive
life

55

The Lost Art of Letters

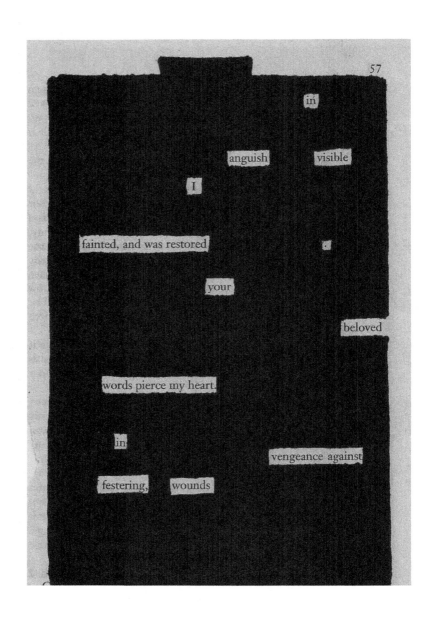

in

anguish   visible

I

fainted, and was restored

your

beloved

words pierce my heart.

in

vengeance against

festering,   wounds

Your Beloved Words

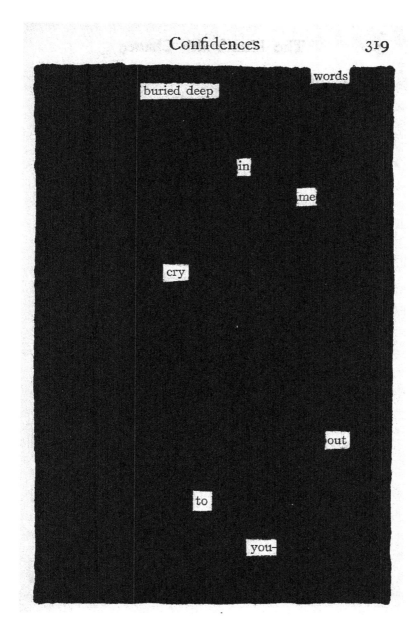

words

buried deep

in

me

cry

out

to

you–

Confidence

197

Acknowledgements

I am enormously grateful to the following:

Joey Anaya, Elias Mennealy, Nicole Wong, Matt Henson-Mayes, Vincent Graham, Ashley Gaines, and everyone at 451 Press and Underwater Mountains Publishing

Austin Kleon, John Carroll, Tyler Knott Gregson, Alicia Cook, and Mary Ruefle for inspiration

All of my Tumblr and Instagram followers

Melissa Buie, Laura Fincher, Sharon Gerald, Lawrence Greene, Rachel Jenkins, Rebecca Kirk, Tammy McPherson, Bethany Sigrest, and Stephanie Woods for their encouragement and advice

Thea Furby, Katie Rogers, and, especially, my mother, Pam Magee, for helping me select the pieces to include in this book

Meg Ainsworth, whose introductory words have lent beauty and legitimacy to the contents of this book

My brother, Robert Magee, for his cover art ideas

My family, especially my parents, Mark and Pam Magee; my grandparents, Robert Ellington and Peggy Magee; Robert, Allison, Avery, and Mallory Magee; and Gerald and Brenda Wells

Most of all, my husband, Chad Wells, for his relentless love and support

A PRIVATE COMPANY

Elias Joseph Mennealy

Ryan Christoper Lutfalah

Christopher Poindexter

CPSIA information can be obtained
at www.ICGtesting.com
Printed in the USA
LVOW04s0908040116

468993LV00010B/239/P